My Big
Fat
Marriage Planner

THE MARRIAGE JOURNEY

THE MARRIAGE ROADMAP

Marriage is not a destination; it is a journey.

1: INTRODUCTION
~ Setting the Scene
~ How to Use the Book
~ Wedding vs. Marriage
~ Joy Vs Happiness
~ Pre-marital Mediation vs.
  Premarital Counselling

2: LEGAL STUFF
(SOUTH AFRICAN LAW)
~ Marital Regimes
~ Prenuptials
~ South African Family Law

3: KNOW THYSELF
~ Characteristics & Values in your spouse
~ Love Languages
~ The Meaning of " I Love You"
~ Love Letter to Myself
~ Conflict Management Techniques
~ Attachment Styles
~ Communication Styles
~ Critical Thinking
~ Personality Assessments
~ Top Ten Reasons for Divorce

4: RELATIONSHIP ASSESSMENT
~ Date Night Questions
~ Marriage & Relationship Questions

5: JOYOUSLY, EVER AFTER
~ Marriage Advice
~ Marriage Strategy
~ SWOT Analysis
~ KPI's and Metrics
~ Wedding Vows
~ Marriage Principles
~ Marriage Manifesto

Do not love half lovers
Do not entertain half friends
Do not indulge in works of the half talented
Do not live half a life
and do not die a half death
If you choose silence, then be silent
When you speak, do so until you are finished
Do not silence yourself to say something
And do not speak to be silent
If you accept, then express it bluntly
Do not mask it
If you refuse then be clear about it
for an ambiguous refusal is but a weak acceptance
Do not accept half a solution
Do not believe half truths
Do not dream half a dream
Do not fantasize about half hopes
Half a drink will not quench your thirst
Half a meal will not satiate your hunger
Half the way will get you no where
Half an idea will bear you no results
Your other half is not the one you love
It is you in another time yet in the same space
It is you when you are not
Half a life is a life you didn't live,
A word you have not said
A smile you postponed
A love you have not had
A friendship you did not know
To reach and not arrive
Work and not work
Attend only to be absent
What makes you a stranger to them closest to you
and they strangers to you
The half is a mere moment of inability
but you are able for you are not half a being
You are a whole that exists to live a life
not half a life

~ Kahlil Gibran

CHAPTER ONE: INTRODUCTION

SETTING THE SCENE

"Being deeply loved by someone gives you strength, while loving someone deeply gives you courage." — Lao Tzu

Consciously and with love, we say "I do", knowing that this knot signifies strengthening the bond between two individuals converging to co-create a beautiful life. Together, we envision the future, rejoicing in the good and tackling the bad with this reinforced promise.

At times, insufficient self-awareness, unaddressed past traumas, and ineffective communication in our marriage can contribute to the development of this intricate web, which, to strengthen our relationship, may grow even more intricate. The realization of your "Happily Ever After" depends on your ability to navigate these complex challenges when facing the everyday tests of life. We should uphold our uniqueness, pursue our aspirations, engage in genuine and transparent dialogues about our shared experiences, and mutually support one another on life's path, collaboratively crafting our journey as we progress.

Nevertheless, there is a need for additional tools and resources to assist us in dealing with conflicts as they emerge. Our default settings encompass our role models, family influences, the narratives we absorb, and the films we observe, among other elements. We require guidance in manoeuvring through these challenging scenarios, so the provision of tools and resources is crucial for effectively handling disputes and tensions.

"My Big Fat Marriage Planner" is a comprehensive resource comprising activities, recommendations, and inspirational poetry drawn from both my personal experiences and my role as a Family Law Mediator.

I've incorporated some of the insights and knowledge gained from my corporate background, experience in Family Law Mediation, and personal life to craft this resource. These tools and frameworks are seldom adapted for use in our relationships, where they have the potential for a significant positive impact. Instead, we often default to our ingrained patterns based on our subconscious behaviours when engaging with our partners in our interpersonal connections.

Applying business methodologies to personal relationships may come across as detached or needing more emotion. On a personal level, metrics provide a framework that can bolster these relationships. While these metrics may not be particularly romantic, they are akin to steering a company. Achieving a successful marriage requires commitment and a focused effort, like running a business. These frameworks aim to simplify the planning process, reducing the need for excessive overthinking when a thoughtful approach is essential for a prosperous marriage.

Establishing a framework minimizes stress and conflicts, allowing for emotional breathing space. By embracing a data-driven approach, you can also engage your emotions more effectively. As time goes by, these structured relationship exercises may become second nature, rendering tracking unnecessary.

The questions and exercises in this manual are designed to help you comprehend challenging situations that may arise in marriage. They aim to foster a deep understanding of your partner before marriage, enabling you to navigate difficult conversations more effectively.

These guidelines and tools introduce structure and reason into a realm where the potent chemistry of love often hampers clear judgment. This guide is designed to aid couples in addressing complex issues by promoting awareness of each other's desires and needs. The questions will guide your thought processes, fostering more efficient conflict resolution through heightened awareness, critical thinking, and problem-solving, ultimately benefitting your marriage.

This guide will help you create a fulfilling marriage in which you become each other's pillars of strength and peace evolving together.

When couples embrace the journey of healing together, upholding honesty, and fostering transparency within their marriage while staying fully conscious, their union will prosper and bring enduring benefits to them, their families, and future generations.

HOW TO USE THIS BOOK

Before taking the plunge into marriage, take the opportunity to connect with your fiancé and delve into deep discussions about your past, present, and future.

You can turn this into an enjoyable experience by either going through the list of questions all in one go during a fun evening or exploring the questions section by section over a few days or weeks.

For optimal benefit from this book, consider the following tips:

Complete the Questionnaire Together:
Start by filling out the questionnaire with your partner.

Self-Reflection and Understanding:
Read each section thoroughly to understand yourself before responding to the questions and completing the Manifesto.

Explore Personality Types and Conflict Styles:
Familiarize yourselves with your Personality Types and Conflict Management Styles. Recognize how these aspects will impact your relationship and leverage this knowledge to build a marriage rooted in awareness, empathy, and understanding.

In-Depth Research and Discussion:
Further investigate the frameworks by taking tests and quizzes online to comprehend your styles and personality types as well as those of your partner. Engage in open, honest conversations surrounding your findings.

Review and Discuss:
After acquiring this additional insight, revisit the questionnaires, complete your responses, and share them with your partner for discussion.
- ♡ You can choose to complete this step in different ways:
- ♡ Share your answers for later discussion.
- ♡ Collaborate in person.
- ♡ Engage with a neutral third party, like a mediator or pre-marital counsellor.

Create a Safe and Open Environment:
Foster a safe space for honesty and vulnerability within your relationship.

Practice Active Listening:
Commit to listening to your future spouse without passing judgment on their responses.

Maintain a Positive Atmosphere:
Keep the process enjoyable and light-hearted.

Stay Present and Focused:
Remain attentive, focused, and in the moment during your discussions.

Express Gratitude:
Thank your future spouse for sharing their thoughts and feelings openly.

Embrace Differences:
Understand that you can have disagreements and still maintain love and respect for each other.

The questions intended for your future spouse are designed to foster connection and intimacy, rather than causing tension or discomfort. These questions serve as conversation initiators, offering couples an opportunity to rediscover each other in a delightful, fresh manner.

This resource can be a valuable tool for identifying shared values, crafting Marriage Values, Vows, and Manifestos, all contributing to a joyful and satisfying marriage.

Furthermore, some of the questions may prove useful in the development of a robust pre-nuptial or ante-nuptial agreement, addressing aspects that you may not have previously considered.

SONNET 116:

LET ME NOT TO THE MARRIAGE OF TRUE MINDS

Let me not to the marriage of true minds
Admit impediments. Love is not love
Which alters when it alteration finds,
Or bends with the remover to remove.
O no! it is an ever-fixed mark
That looks on tempests and is never shaken;
It is the star to every wand'ring bark,
Whose worth's unknown, although his height be taken.
Love's not time's fool, though rosy lips and cheeks
Within his bending sickle's compass come;
Love alters not with his brief hours and weeks,
But bears it out even to the edge of doom.
If this be error and upon me prov'd,
I never writ, nor no man ever lov'd.

~ William Shakespeare

THE DIFFERENCE BETWEEN THE WEDDING AND THE MARRIAGE

Let us begin by exploring the distinction between "The Wedding" and "The Marriage."

When we embrace the fairy tale ideals that have been instilled in our minds since childhood, our focus shifts towards preparing for the wedding day rather than the marriage itself. Our subconscious fixates so heavily on the dreamy wedding that our life's purpose and journey become centred around that event: creating the perfect family, raising children, acquiring a mortgage, and the quintessential home with a white picket fence. However, it's crucial to recognize that fairy tales typically end at the point of the wedding, with the Prince and Princess getting married, sharing a kiss, and living "Happily Ever After."

Here's the less popular perspective: Love alone is insufficient. Achieving "Ever After" is a complex endeavour. Love is an action, not a passive state. It demands intention, effort, and a continuous commitment to remain in love. Achieving "Ever After" requires consistent, deliberate work.

Marriage is where reality takes hold, and it can be challenging to shift our mindset in the first couple of years to the concept of being married. Beyond the wedding day is where love's true nature is tested and understood.

All the great romances in literature, stories, and movies—classics included—rarely delve into the concept of marriage and enduring commitment. Dealing with the ups and downs, ebbs, and flows of life is not prominently showcased in works like Shakespeare's "Romeo and Juliet" or "The Titanic." However, Othello does reveal the potential darkness that can emerge in the human psyche when communication in a marriage breaks down.

The statistics are not in your favour. The numbers are staggering, and undeniably, the leading cause of divorce is...Marriage.

So, marry, but do so with self-awareness, awakening, and consciousness. Planning your relationship and your future may seem like it could diminish the romance, but take it from me, a divorcee, a family law mediator, and a woman who still believes in love and romance despite it all: it's better to prepare for what lies ahead.

The questions and ideas presented in this guide will help you navigate the rollercoaster of love and better understand how to make your marriage work beyond the wedding and honeymoon phases. These tough questions should be asked, answered, and addressed.

As much intention, energy, and enthusiasm should be invested in planning the marriage as in planning the wedding. While planning the marriage is a more prolonged, ongoing, and, at times messy process, the hard work will undoubtedly pay off.

Let us strive for a joyful union as two individuals who come together to grow and thrive together. Think of it as an investment in a well-lived life. Think of it as an investment in your **"Joyously, Ever After."**

JOY VERSUS HAPPINESS

Perhaps we should strive for our **"Joyously, Ever, After"** instead of **"Happily, Ever, After."**

Let me tell you why.

"Joy seems a step beyond happiness—happiness is a sort of atmosphere you can live in sometimes when you're lucky. Joy is a light that fills you with hope and faith, and love." - Adela Rogers St. Johns, Some Are Born Great

Let us look at the differences between Joy and Happiness.

Table 1 - Happiness Versus Joy

Happiness	Joy
Result of an external force that brings satisfaction to us	Result of inner peace and satisfaction
Source of happiness that is external	The source of joy is within ourselves
It has a more materialistic attribute to it	It has a moral attribute to it
The outcome may be a mutual understanding, strengthening of our bonds with others, admiration etc	The outcome is self-realisation and supreme satisfaction
Not that consistent since it typically depends on an external force that brings happiness to us	More consistent and long-lasting

1*

Table 2 - The differences between happiness and joy

	Happiness	Joy
Meaning	Happiness is when one experiences feelings ranging from contentment and satisfaction to bliss and intense pleasure.	Joy is a more substantial, less common feeling than happiness. Witnessing or achieving selflessness to the point of personal sacrifice frequently triggers this emotion. Feeling spiritually connected to a God or to people.
Causes	Earthly experiences, material objects	Spiritual experiences, caring for others, gratitude, thankfulness
Emotion	An outward expression of elation	Inward peace and contentment
Time Frame	Temporary, based on outward circumstances	Lasting, based on inward circumstances
Example	Amid life's ups and downs, happiness is still present.	Serving others, sometimes through sacrifice with no possible personal gain. Witnessing justice for the less fortunate. Feeling close to a God.
Analogy	Happiness is a state. Think of it as a 100-story building and each level corresponds to a happiness value. And that happiness will persist for quite a long time	Joy is that sudden burst of happiness. Joy is like the elevator in that building that takes you up to higher levels of happiness only for a small amount of time and back.
Life	Happiness can be experienced from any good activity, food or company.	Joy is a by product of a moral lifestyle.

2*

PRE-MARITAL MEDIATION

Event preparations such as guest lists, invitations, floral arrangements, menu selection, and photographer bookings are common components of wedding planning. However, an increasing number of couples are now including a "pre-nuptial or pre-marital agreement" on their wedding planning agenda. This trend is driven by the fact that many couples are tying the knot at a later stage in life or embarking on a second marriage, and they recognize the need to safeguard their assets and future, acknowledging the statistical reality that many marriages may eventually lead to divorce.

Primarily, it's important to clarify that pre-marital mediation and agreements extend beyond individuals who either "lack trust in their partner" or "have substantial assets to safeguard." Many individuals fail to engage in essential conversations with their future spouse before marriage, leading to challenges in addressing crucial aspects like financial matters, child-rearing, and other significant topics. There's no avoiding it: pre-marital mediation serves as a cornerstone for fostering open communication, trust, and transparency in your impending marriage, regardless of the circumstances.

Marriage presents its challenges, yet it also offers moments of immense joy. To navigate the difficulties and savour the wonderful moments, it's essential to establish a strong foundation. This foundation ensures that when faced with tough times, both partners remain committed and don't contemplate walking away.

Mediating a pre-nuptial agreement can provide a compassionate and considerate method for addressing the sometimes-awkward topic of an uncertain future. Enlisting the support of an unbiased third party to guide you through complex discussions can contribute to a more secure relationship and a deeper comprehension of your partner.

Pre-marital mediation empowers couples to collaboratively craft a mutually satisfactory agreement. Additionally, it provides an opportunity for couples to acquire valuable communication skills that will continue to benefit their marriage.

If you're interested in pursuing pre-nuptial mediation, the questions within this book can guide you through a more in-depth exploration of these topics.

Often, the following topics are covered in pre-marital mediation.

- Pre-Marital Assets and Debts
- Marital Property
- Management of Assets and Income
- Spousal or Child Support
- Credit and Debt
- Working
- Gifts and Inheritance from families
- Taxes
- Higher Education
- Duration of Pre-marital Agreement
- Business Ownership
- Fault – Cause of the divorce - *South Africa has a no-fault divorce system, but aspects relating to forfeiture due to misconduct can be noted.

3*

PRE-MARITAL MEDIATION VS PRE-MARITAL COUNSELLING

What are the differences between pre-marital mediation and pre-marital counselling? Now, let's explore this in more detail.

Pre-marital mediation elements:

A Strong Marriage Foundation:
Pre-marital mediation helps couples prepare and plan for a long-lasting, successful marriage.

Ensuring Marital Alignment:
The conversation puts you on the same page before you get married, so you stay on the same page.

Enhances Proactive Communication:
Improves communication on important issues like finances, communication and conflict styles, family relationships, pet peeves, values and planning a family.

Formulating Financial Terms for Marriage:
Mediation is when the two upcoming spouses meet with a neutral mediator to discuss and formulate the financial terms of their forthcoming marriage.

The Three-Step Mediation Process:
It's a three-way process where the mediator obtains the facts with guided questions and aspects of the relationship that are important to both parties and facilitates a discussion between the parties of terms they agree on.

Impartial Mediators:
Impartial, qualified Mediators are qualified to "level the playing field." In the prenup context, this primarily means eliciting the views and concerns of each spouse in a safe environment where all problems can safely be raised and addressed.

Expertise in Problem Solving:
An experienced pre-nuptial agreement mediator can lead the parties towards solutions they (and their attorneys) may not have thought about.

PRE-MARITAL COUNSELLING

Preparing for a wedding is merely the beginning of preparing for a marriage. As much as wedding preparations take time and effort, so does marriage preparation! Often, couples are too busy preparing themselves to be the groom and bride that they overlook preparing themselves to be husband and wife.

A good marriage needs a good foundation. The best time to start marriage preparation is when you and your partner have begun thinking about marital commitment. Premarital counselling is a therapy that helps prepare couples mentally for marriage. Counselling helps ensure that you and your spouse can have a strong and healthy relationship throughout your life. Premarital counselling helps to improve a couple's relationship before marriage.

Partners often choose each other for reasons that are not fully conscious; it is only with further processing that they may understand how familiar aspects of their partner relate to unresolved conflicts in the past.

Premarital counselling often requires you and your partner to complete a questionnaire separately to determine how you feel about one another and what you expect from your relationship. These questionnaires can help your counsellor identify your strengths, weaknesses, areas of compatibility, and potential problem areas.

Premarital counselling can also involve identifying and exploring significant life events and early childhood experiences, which impact the relationship and how each partner relates to the other.

WHY EMBARK ON PREMARITAL COUNSELLING?

Pre-marital counselling offers an opportunity to discuss several important aspects of a marriage, including (but not limited to):

❤️ **Finances:**
Money can be stressful and contentious for married couples, so deciding how to manage your finances in advance can help prevent problems.

❤️ **Beliefs, values, and religion:**
Sharing your beliefs, values, and religious sentiments with your partner can help foster better understanding and respect. You can also discuss the implications of these aspects in your daily life.

❤️ **Roles in the marriage:**
It's essential to discuss the roles you expect yourself and your partner to play in your marriage to prevent conflicts later on.

❤️ **Activities and time spent together:**
You and your partner can discuss how you plan to spend time together and what activities you enjoy.

❤️ **Children:**
Couples sometimes realize after getting married that they are not on the same page about whether they want to have children. Deciding in advance whether you wish to have kids and how you want to raise them is essential.

❤️ **Family relationships:**
Premarital counselling can allow you to be honest about your relationships with your own family and any concerns about your partner's family.

Pre-marital counselling is designed to equip you and your partner with tools to navigate married life together.

These are some of the benefits this therapy can offer:

💜 **Learn constructive communication:**
A core aspect of premarital counselling is communication, as partners learn to convey their positions clearly without attacking or arming the other.

💜 **Develop conflict resolution skills:**
Teaches you and your partner problem-solving and conflict-resolution skills. Initially, communication often leads to conflict, but couples can have more constructive discussions with time.

💜 **Focus on the positive aspects:**
This can help you and your partner focus on the positive aspects of your relationship rather than the negative.

💜 **Eliminate dysfunctional behaviour:**
This can identify unhealthy behaviours and patterns in a relationship and help you correct them.

💜 **Build decision-making processes:**
This can help you and your partner develop healthy and equitable decision-making processes

💜 **Alleviate fears related to marriage:**
If you or your partner are anxious about what married life will entail, premarital counselling can help you discuss important issues and give you some clarity.

4*

ON LOVE

When love beckons to you, follow him,
Though his ways are hard and steep.
And when his wings enfold you yield to him,
Though the sword hidden among his
pinions may wound you.

And when he speaks to you believe in him,
Though his voice may shatter your dreams
as the north wind lays waste the garden.
For even as love crowns you so shall he
crucify you.

Even as he is for your growth.
so is he for your pruning.
Even as he ascends to your height and
caresses your tenderest branches that quiver in the sun,
So shall he descend to your roots and
shake them in their clinging to the earth.

Like sheaves of corn, he gathers you unto himself.
He threshes you to make you naked.
He sifts you to free you from your husks.
He grinds you to whiteness.
He kneads you until you are pliant.
And then he assigns you to his sacred
fire, that you may become sacred bread for
God's sacred feast.

All these things shall love to do unto you
that you may know the secrets of your
heart, and in that knowledge become a
fragment of life's heart.

But if in your fear you would seek only
love's peace and love's pleasure,
Then it is better for you that you cover
your nakedness and pass out of love's threshing-floor,
Into the seasonless world where you
shall laugh, but not all of your laughter,
and weep, but not all of your tears.

Love gives naught but itself and takes naught but from itself.
Love possesses not nor would it be possessed.
For love is sufficient unto love.

When you love you should not say,
"God is in my heart," but rather,
"I am in the heart of God."
And think not you can direct the course of love,
for love, if it finds you worthy, directs your course.

Love has no other desire but to fulfil itself.
But if you love and must needs have
desires, let these be your desires:
To melt and be like a running brook
that sings its melody to the night.

To know the pain of too much tenderness.
To be wounded by your own under-standing of love.
And to bleed willingly and joyfully.
To wake at dawn with a winged heart
and give thanks for another day of loving.
To rest at the noon hour and meditate
love's ecstasy.
To return home at eventide with gratitude.
And then to sleep with a prayer for the
beloved in your heart and a song of praise
upon your lips.

~ Kahlil Gibran

CHAPTER TWO: LEGAL STUFF
(SOUTH AFRICAN LAW)

PREPARING TO GET MARRIED

"A successful marriage requires falling in love many times, always with the same person."
- Mignon McLaughlin

I may not be aware of your location while you read and engage with this guide, but I strongly recommend familiarizing yourself with the marital laws in your country before you embark on marriage.

Legal regulations safeguard your rights as an individual since you're entering a legally binding contract with the presumption of mental competence. In South African law, the Latin term "Caveat Subscriptor" serves as a cautionary reminder to the signatory to exercise awareness.

South African law recognises three types of marriages: **civil marriages, customary marriages, and civil unions.**

The solemnisation and registration of civil marriages, customary marriages and civil unions are managed by the Department of Home Affairs.

- **Civil marriages are governed by the Marriage Act and regulations issued in terms of the Act.**
  Civil Marriages are performed by a marriage officer at a Home Affairs office and are governed by the Marriage Act of 1961. These marriages are typically secular and do not require religious or cultural traditions.

- **Customary Marriages are governed by the Recognition of Customary Marriages Act of 1998**
  Customary Marriages are recognized as valid if they follow the customs and traditions of the parties involved. These marriages may involve exchanging gifts or paying lobola (bride price) and may be conducted by a traditional leader or elder.

- **Civil unions are recognised in terms of the Civil Union Act (2006).**
  Civil Unions, also known as same-sex marriages, are governed by the Civil Union Act of 2006, allowing same-sex couples to enter a legally recognized union. These unions are performed by a marriage officer and offer the same rights and responsibilities as a civil marriage.

NOTE: If you are planning on getting married, you must:

♥ Ensure that you are legally allowed to marry.

♥ Understand the legal consequences of a marriage, particularly that marriages in South Africa are automatically in community of property, unless a valid ante-nuptial contract has been entered into before the marriage, and

♥ Make sure that your marriage will comply with all the legal requirements for a valid marriage.

♥ Should you be unsure of any of these, legal counsel should be sought before the marriage is entered.

5*

The Marital Regimes in South Africa

In South Africa, the matrimonial regimes of married couples are primarily regulated by the Matrimonial Property Act (88 of 1984), which provides for three different matrimonial regimes, namely:

- ❤ **In Community of Property (COP).**

- ❤ **Out of Community of Property (OCOP); and**

- ❤ **Out of Community of Property with the accrual system.**

Each of the matrimonial regimes and their most essential characteristics are as per below:

IN COMMUNITY OF PROPERTY

The first matrimonial regime is marriage In Community of Property.

The default position in South African law at the time of creating this guide, is that a marriage is concluded in community of property. When a couple fail to conclude a valid ante-nuptial agreement before their wedding day, they will automatically be married in Community of Property.

This matrimonial regime entails that the separate estates of the partners, which they built up prior to their marriage, now become one estate for all legal purposes.

Prior to Marriage	After Marriage
Partner 1's Estate: • R100 000 assets • R20 000 debt	**Joint Estate:** • R150 000 assets • R35 000 debt
Partner 2's Estate: • R50 000 assets • R15 000 debt	

After their marriage, the couple have one combined estate in which each is a 50% owner. The property and assets that belonged to Partner 1 prior to the marriage (except for certain instances such as property or assets that were inherited) is now 50% owned by Partner 2 and vice versa.

Seeing that the couple no longer have any separate estates but one joint estate, each party's debt before the marriage also becomes the debt of the other party after the marriage.

Therefore, engaged couples must be open and honest about their financial situation before the wedding day, as it may severely impact the other party.

The advantage of a marriage in community of property was traditionally seen as a protection of the partner's interests, who stayed at home and raised children, while the other partner was involved in commerce and increasingly gained income.

In the event of the partner's death or a divorce, the stay-at-home partner would be entitled to 50% of their joint estate. This would therefore avoid a situation where the stay-at-home partner, after all the years working in the family home and raising children, is left without money.

THE DISADVANTAGES OF A MARRIAGE IN COMMUNITY OF PROPERTY

The couple no longer has separate estates, and both must give their written consent for certain commercial transactions, amongst others:

💜 **Purchasing or selling an immovable property.**

💜 **Signing surety.**

💜 **Entering into a credit agreement as a "consumer" where the National Credit Act (2005) is applicable.**

💜 **Alienating or pledging jewellery, coins, stamps, paintings, or any other assets of the joint estate and held mainly as investments.**

However, some of these requirements may not be applicable if one of the spouses enters such transactions in the ordinary course of their trade, profession or business.

A spouse may not institute legal proceedings against any other person or defend such pro-ceedings without the consent of the other spouse, except for legal proceedings in respect of their separate property, for the recovery of damages (other than patrimonial loss) or in respect of a matter about their trade, profession, or business.

Similarly, if an application for the sequestration of one spouse is brought, it is brought against both, and the joint estate is sequestrated, and both the husband and the wife will be declared insolvent.

Although a couple may be married in community of property, it is nevertheless possible for them to own property or assets that do not fall within their joint estate, known as their "separate property", for instance, any inheritance bequeathed to a spouse.

OUT OF COMMUNITY OF PROPERTY
(ANTE-NUPTIAL CONTRACT – ANC)

The second matrimonial regime is a marriage out of community of property.

To be married out of community of property, the couple must conclude a valid ante-nuptial agreement prior to their wedding day.

The ante-nuptial agreement is signed (executed) before a Notary Public (attorney) and registered at the relevant Deeds Office. Verifying the Registration at the Deeds Office is very important as many couples find out later that their ANC was not registered at the Deeds Office, and they are then recorded as married in community of property which can have adverse effects later.

This matrimonial regime entails that the husband and wife each retain their separate estates after the conclusion of their marriage.

Whatever each of the parties owned before the marriage remains their sole and exclusive property after the marriage and vice versa. The same applies to those assets and property acquired by each party during their marriage.

Upon the death of one of the spouses or a divorce, the other spouse will have no claim against any portion of the other spouse's estate (except to the extent that a claim for maintenance may still exist).

This matrimonial regime is most prevalent where a husband and wife have already built substantial estates before marriage or spouses conduct their own businesses.

Some of the advantages of this matrimonial regime are the following:

💙 Each spouse retains their estate, therefore the creditors of one spouse have no rights or claims against the property or estate of the other spouse's estate.

💙 Each spouse is free to conduct business, enter transactions and acquire assets and property without the cooperation or consent of the other spouse.

💙 Where one of the spouses is sequestrated, it does not affect the other spouse, who continues to carry on independently of the insolvent spouse.

💜 Even though the couple have separate estates, each has a statutory obligation to contribute to the necessities of their household pro rata to their financial means.

💜 Spouses are also jointly and severally liable to third parties for any debts incurred by either of them for the necessaries of their joint household.

OUT OF COMMUNITY WITH THE ACCRUAL SYSTEM (ANC WITH ACCRUAL)

The third matrimonial regime is a marriage out of community of property with the accrual system.

As with a marriage out of community of property as discussed above, the parties must execute a proper ante-nuptial agreement before their wedding day.

Unless a couple explicitly excludes the operation of the accrual system in their ante-nuptial agreement, the accrual system will automatically apply to their marriage out of community of property.

What the accrual system entails is that at the dissolution of a marriage by divorce or by the death of one or both spouses, the spouse whose estate shows no accrual or a smaller accrual than the estate of the other spouse, obtains a claim against the other spouse or his estate for an amount equal to 50% of the difference between the accrual of the respective estates of the spouses.

This is a simplified example to illustrate this principle:

Estate values at date of marriage	Estate values at dissolution of marriage
Partner 1's Estate: • R100 000 assets	**Partner 1's Estate:** • R1 000 000 assets
Partner 2's Estate: • R50 000 assets	**Partner 2's Estate:** • R200 000 assets
Difference in Value = R 50 000	**Difference in growth = R 750 000**

In this example, Partner 1's estate grew R900 000 in value from the date of conclusion of the marriage to the date of dissolution of the marriage. Partner 2's estate only grew by R150 000 for the same period.

The difference in the growth between Partner 1 and Partner 2's estates is, therefore, R750 000.

Upon dissolution of the marriage, the person whose estate had no, or the least growth obtains a claim against the other spouse or his estate for 50% of the difference between the growth in their respective estates.

In our example, Partner 2's estate had the least growth. They will therefore have a claim against Partner 1's or his/her estate (in the event of their death) for R375 000, 50% of the difference in growth between their respective estates.

The spouses must specify the commencement value of their respective estates in their ante-nuptial agreement to make it easier to calculate their growth accurately.

In our example above, Partner 2 will state his/her commencement value as R50 000 and Partner 1 as R100 000. If they both start with a value of R0.00, the value of everything each of them owns at the date that they enter the marriage will immediately be considered as "growth" in their respective estates for determining accrual.

The parties to a marriage out of community of property with the accrual system can exclude some or all their assets from the accrual system in their ante-nuptial agreement.

Partner 2 may for instance wish to exclude all his/her jewellery and the family farm that he/she inherited from his/her father. The value of these assets will then not be considered when determining the value of the growth in his/her estate.

This can be illustrated as follows:

If the couple decided to specify their starting values at R0.00.

The jewellery is worth R50 000, and the family farm is R1 000 000.

If the jewellery and family farm is not expressly excluded from the accrual in the ante-nuptial agreement, then the growth in Partner 2's estate will be R1 050 000 immediately after the marriage.

During a marriage to which the accrual system applies, the right of a spouse to share in the accrual of the estate of the other spouse is not transferable or liable to attachment. Also, it does not form part of the insolvent estate of a spouse. The accrual claim is safe from a spouse's creditors.

Any inheritance, legacy or donation received by a spouse during their marriage will not form part of the accrual unless the spouses agree to it.

The accrual of a deceased spouse's estate is determined before any testamentary disposition, donation upon death or intestate succession takes place.

This section protects the surviving spouse in that the value of the accrual of the deceased spouse's estate must be determined before any inheritance is paid out to any person.

TAX CONSIDERATIONS

It is recommended that married couples consult professional financial planners to assist them with structuring their estates to avoid paying unnecessary taxes and estate duties upon the death of a spouse.

One crucial aspect that needs to be addressed already in the antenuptial agreement of the married couple is the entitlement of the surviving spouse or children of the deceased to receive the amount due under a life insurance policy.

In terms of Section 3(3)(a)(i) of the Estate Duty Act (45 of 1955), the amount due under such policy that is recoverable by the surviving spouse or child of the deceased under a duly registered ante-nuptial or post-nuptial contract is not considered for purposes of calculating the value of the deceased estate for estate duty purposes.

The exclusion of the value of any life insurance policy payable to the surviving spouse or children of a deceased for calculating the value of a deceased estate could have a massive impact on the amount of estate duty that will be payable upon a deceased spouse's death. Therefore, ensure that this aspect is appropriately regulated in the antenuptial agreement where the parties will be married out of community of property (with or without the accrual system).

WILL AND BENEFICIARY UPDATES

It is important to ensure that you update your will to reflect what will occur in the event of any one or both party's death. This should include guardianship of the children.

All policies and investment beneficiaries should also be updated. Consult a professional to assist you with this, especially if you have a large estate which includes various assets and asset classes.

PRE-NUPTIAL AGREEMENTS

As you plan your **"Joyously, Ever After"**, a little something might await your legal attention: a pre-nuptial or ante-nuptial agreement.

Many couples tend to steer clear of prenuptial discussions due to their fear of invoking the word "divorce." However, initiating a conversation about a pre-nuptial agreement doesn't cast any negative influence on the prospects of a "Joyously Ever After." The concept behind a pre-nuptial agreement is to safeguard the interests of both parties and their assets.

Like how you would protect your possessions against potential risks, whether they occur or not, you should also safeguard your interests within your marriage. A pre-nuptial agreement accomplishes this very purpose.

What is a Pre-nuptial Agreement (Prenup)?

Two people sign a pre-nuptial agreement before they get married, a legally binding contract that addresses all financial issues involved in the marriage.

The "prenup" will address financial aspects such as property brought in by each party, property acquired during the marriage and what decisions will be made regarding the division and ownership of the property.

Although it may not be the most 'romantic' thing to do, this honest financial discussion can positively affect your relationship. It also allows you to discuss how you will deal with your financial situation throughout your marriage – if you have not already discussed this.

So how do you know if a pre-nuptial agreement suits you as a couple?

Creating and signing a prenup does not mean that you are planning to get a divorce. Pre-nuptial contracts go a long way to preserve family ties, inheritance, and children's financial well-being from previous marriages. Moreover, this kind of agreement can cover spousal support obligations, the children's educational obligations, and the parties' financial obligations.

Personal and business assets accrued before your marriage are protected, and a prenup will also state how the assets will be divided in the event of death. In a divorce, a prenup eliminates any battles over assets and money.

Fair warning: *Prenups are known to cause friction in relationships and among extended family, especially if an inheritance is involved. These agreements can create the impression that there is a lack of trust between partners and can create resentment, especially when one party has more financial wealth than the other. Ideally, it is a good idea to have Pre-Marital Mediation when creating a pre-nuptial agreement, especially if there are signs of conflict.*

Pre-nuptial Agreements are not necessary for all couples, especially if no one brings any significant assets into the marriage. Speak openly with your partner, parents, or anyone you trust to get their opinion before you make your final decision.

The most common reasons for entering into a Pre-nuptial Agreement are:

- The parties do not want to be held liable for debts that the other spouse incurred before or during their marriage.

- They want to protect their assets from creditors, especially when they own businesses.

- They do not want certain assets to form part of a joint estate.

- They want to be able to enter transactions without the other spouse's consent.

- They want to control their properties, estates, and debts.

SOUTH AFRICAN FAMILY LAW

Family or matrimonial law incorporates family matters and domestic relationships such as marriage and civil unions, divorce and annulment, child custody and the child's best interests, maintenance, child abuse and domestic violence. You must understand the relevant legislation in your country, state or province, wherever you are in the world so that you make informed decisions when entering into a marriage contract.

When it comes to establishing or terminating a marriage contract in South Africa, various pieces of legislation should be considered. The applicability of these laws depends on how the contract was initiated and the specific circumstances of the relationship. It is recommended to seek the assistance of a qualified practitioner when entering or dissolving a marriage contract. This ensures that all your rights, responsibilities, and any considerations related to future children (if applicable) are properly addressed.

Marriage Laws

- 💗 Marriage Act 25 of 1961
- 💗 Civil Union Act 17 of 2006
- 💗 Recognition of Customary Marriages Act 120 of 1998
- 💗 Maintenance of Surviving Spouse Act
- 💗 Matrimonial Property Act 88 of 1984

Children's Rights

- 💗 Children's Act 38 of 2005
- 💗 Maintenance Act 99 of 1998
- 💗 Child Justice Act 2008
- 💗 Hague Convention on International Child Abduction

Children's Rights

- 💗 Divorce Act 70 of 1979
- 💗 Domicile Act 3 of 1992
- 💗 Domestic Partnership Bill
- 💗 Domestic Violence Act 116 of 1998 | Domestic Violence Amendment Act 2021
- 💗 Intestate Succession Act 81 of 1987
- 💗 Wills Act 7 of 1953

LOVE ONE ANOTHER

"Love one another,
but make not a bond of love:
let it rather be a moving sea
between the shores of your souls.
fill each other's cup
but drink not from one cup.
give one another of your bread
but eat not from the same loaf
sing and dance together and be joyous,
but let each one of you be alone,
even as the strings of a lute are alone
though they quiver with the same music."

~ Kahlil Gibran

CHAPTER THREE: KNOW THYSELF

CHARACTERISTICS AND VALUES OF MY SPOUSE

Knowing yourself is the beginning of all wisdom - Aristotle.

Have you ever taken a moment to contemplate the qualities you desire in your future partner? It's a common understanding that nobody is flawless, and the likelihood of finding a partner who perfectly embodies your every dream might be slim, but it's not impossible.

How can you recognize if you've found that special someone if you haven't clearly defined what you're seeking in a spouse?

What are the key criteria and priorities guiding your choice when it comes to selecting a life partner?

Start by asking yourself these basic questions:

⏰   What do I want in a spouse?

⏰   How do I want them to look physically?

⏰   What are their values?

⏰   How do their values align with mine?

⏰   What are my pet peeves, my likes, and dislikes – Good and Bad Habits, Hygiene and Cleanliness

⏰   What are my Top Priorities, non-negotiable characteristics, and values?

⏰   What are compromises I am willing to make?

EXAMPLES OF CHARACTERISTICS AND VALUES

Each person comes into a relationship with their biases, paradigms, judgements, understanding, and view of the world around them.

When you list a characteristic or value, elaborate on what it means. How does this show up for you, and what that look, sounds, or feels like to you?

Everyone will have their idea of what each of these means. Still, unless you can articulate what it means for you, it may always remain ambiguous to the other party, remaining unfulfilled and being a cause of conflict.

What is good vs bad values?

Good values can be:	Bad values can be:
Reality Based	Superstitious
Socially constructive	Socially destructive
Immediate and Controllable	Not immediate or controllable.

6*

Some examples of good, healthy values are honesty, innovative, vulnerable, standing up for oneself and others. Self-respect, curiosity, charitable, humble, creative.

Bad values generally rely on external events whereas good values can be achieved internally. Values, however, are about prioritization.

What are the values that you prioritise above all else and therefore influence your decision making above all else.

If you decide that you want someone that is a "Great communicator", you will need to articulate that means to you e.g. I want a partner who communicates and knows how to express their feelings, desires, and needs.

If you cannot articulate what you want in a spouse, you may always fail to accurately communicate your needs to your partner, which can result in conflict.

Here are some more examples that you can use and elaborate on:

💗 Wants to spend quality time with me – What is quality time to you? How often, doing what?

💗 Makes our relationship a priority – *What will they do or say to you for you to know that your relationship is a priority and a priority over what else?*

💗 Growth Mindset

💗 Intellectual

💗 Humility

💗 Sexy, Tall, Fit and Toned

💗 Growth Mindset

💗 Neat and clean, hygiene is essential.

💗 Loyal and Trustworthy

💗 Ambitious

- ❤️ Great leadership qualities
- ❤️ Loves what they do as a career.
- ❤️ Funny. Makes me laugh.
- ❤️ Shares Core Values
- ❤️ Able to communicate with emotional maturity around areas of conflict.
- ❤️ Responds and communicates feelings instead of reacting to anger.
- ❤️ Teaches me new things and likes to try new things.
- ❤️ Be able to learn and grow together.
- ❤️ We go on adventures together.
- ❤️ Respects me
- ❤️ Must have Emotional Maturity
- ❤️ Forgiving
- ❤️ Compassionate and empathetic
- ❤️ Patient and kind
- ❤️ Affirms me and is my greatest supporter.
- ❤️ Loves children.
- ❤️ My friends and family love and respects him, and he loves and respects them.
- ❤️ Loves Pets
- ❤️ Love to travel with me.
- ❤️ Shares a love for food.
- ❤️ Sees and acknowledges me.

I HAVE BECOME THE GIVER OF LIGHT

i was dead, i came alive
i was tears, i became laughter
all because of love when it arrived
my temporal life from then on
changed to eternal

love said to me
you are not crazy enough
you don't fit this house

i went and became crazy
crazy enough to be in chains
love said you are not
intoxicated enough
you don't fit the group

i went and got drunk
drunk enough to overflow
with light-headedness
love said you are still too clever
filled with imagination and skepticism

i went and became gullible
and in fright pulled away from it all
love said
you are a candle attracting everyone
gathering every one around you

i am no more
a candle spreading light
i gather no more crowds
and like smoke
i am all scattered now

love said
you are a teacher you are a head
and for everyone you are a leader
i am no more
not a teacher, not a leader
just a servant to your wishes

love said
you already have your own wings
i will not give you more feathers
and then my heart pulled itself apart
and filled to the brim with a new light
overflowed with fresh life

now even the heavens are thankful that
because of love i have become
the giver of light

~ Rumi

LOVE LANGUAGES

Frequent conflicts can emerge when individuals express love in distinct ways. One person might demonstrate affection through gifts and acts of service, while the other prefers physical touch. When we fail to understand each other's love languages, it leads to miscommunication of our affection, ultimately leading to relationship discord.

There are five love languages, first introduced in 1992 by marriage counsellor Dr Gary Chapman in his book "The 5 Love Languages."

The five love languages are:

- Words of affirmation
- Quality time
- Physical touch
- Acts of service
- Receiving gifts

P.S. Love languages don't just apply to romantic relationships. They can be helpful in your platonic relationships, too.

Table 3 - Understanding Love Languages

Love Language	Associated with	It might be your's if	If this sounds like a partner
Words of Affirmation	Verbal expressions of love, appreciation, and encouragement	You like hearing "I love you" often, you thrive when you're encouraged by others	Say — and mean — more I love you's, thank you's, you matter to me's
Quality Time	Giving another person your undivided attention	You make time for others; you feel disconnected when you don't spend enough time together	Have date nights, turn off your phones when you're together, sit together and talk about your days
Physical Touch	Connection through appropriate physical touch (nonsexual or sexual)	You're a "touchy-feely" person, you feel most loved when embraced or touched	Hold hands, be generous with affection. Prioritise sex if it's important in the relationship
Acts of service	Selfless, thoughtful acts that make a person's life easier	You're happy when someone helps without being asked, actions speak louder than words for you	Make them meals, take on a chore or two around the house, draw them baths
Receiving gifts	Tangible tokens of love and thoughtfulness	You pride yourself on giving thoughtful gifts, you most appreciate meaningful gifts	Surprise them with gifts outside of special occasions, bring home their favourite treat, buy or make them that are personal

Finding out yours and your partners love language will help you with many areas of conflict throughout your relationship. Access free quizzes online to help you with this exercise.

7*

HOW TO SPEAK YOUR PARTNER'S LOVE LANGUAGE

According to your love language, there exist various approaches for action, specific deeds to undertake, behaviours to steer clear of, and conflict resolution strategies at your disposal. Here are some illustrative examples to guide you.

Table 4 - Speaking your partners love language.

Love Language	How to Communicate	Actions to Take	Things to Avoid	After Conflict
Words of Affirmation	Encourage, Affirm, appreciate, and listen actively	Send an unexpected note, or text. Verbal compliments that express love and appreciation e.g., a love letter	Not recognising or appreciating effort	Speak words that build security and give sincere apologies
Quality Time	Focused and undivided attention spent together	Turn off electronics, plan date nights, go for a walk, do a hobby together, weekend getaways	Distractions when spending time together, long stints without one-on-one time	Make eye contact, active listening with empathy, don't interrupt
Physical Touch	Nonverbal, use body language and touch to emphasise love	Long hugs, gentle caressing, kissing, hugging, hand holding, massages, making intimacy a priority	Physical neglect, long stints without intimacy, receiving affection coldly	Hold each other, cuddle together in bed
Acts of service	Any act that eases burden or responsibility. Knowing that you are with them to help or partner with them	Breakfast in bed, pamper them, or do chores together. Alleviate their workload or do things for them that they may think cumbersome	Making the requests of others a priority Lacking follow through on tasks big and small	Make behaviour changes on items that cause conflict

Love Language	How to Communicate	Actions to Take	Things to Avoid	After Conflict
Receiving gifts	Tangible symbols that reflect thoughtfulness and effort	Make birthdays and big events special. Give thoughtful things and gestures. Small things matter in a big way. Give gratitude when receiving a gift.	Forgetting special occu-sions, giving gifts unenthusiastical-ly or not putting thought into the gift	Give a small token of your love and an apology note

WRITE DOWN YOUR LOVE LANGUAGES

....

....

....

....

....

....

....

....

....

....

....

....

....

....

....

WRITE DOWN HOW YOU WOULD LIKE YOUR PARTNER TO COMMUNICATE IN YOUR LOVE LANGUAGE TO YOU

ADVISE YOUR PARTNER ON THINGS TO AVOID

I LOVE YOU MORE

When I say

I LOVE YOU more, I don't mean

I LOVE YOU more than you love me. I mean

I LOVE YOU more than the bad days ahead of us.

I LOVE YOU more than any fight we will ever have.

I LOVE YOU more than the distance between us.

I LOVE YOU more than any obstacle that could ever try and come between us.

I LOVE YOU the most.

~ UNKNOWN

THE MEANING OF "I LOVE YOU"

What does "I Love You" Mean to Me?

When you say "I Love You" to someone, what does that mean to you? When they say "I Love You" to you, what does that mean to you?

What does it mean to them?

Often, we say "I Love You" with an expectation that our partner knows what that means. Sometimes "I Love You", and its meaning gets diluted, and we forget the power of the words because we fail to articulate what it means for me when I say "I Love You" to you.

Here is an example of what "I Love You" means. I urge you to articulate this to your spouse so that they know what it means to you when you say these three powerful words.

When I Say, "I Love You," I mean:

💜 I will always be your biggest supporter and number one fan.

💜 I will always be in your corner.

💜 I will be honest no matter how difficult the conversations get.

💜 I will call you out on your limiting beliefs for you to be the best version of yourself.

💜 I will be respectful. You see me, and I see you.

💜 I commit to healing and growing with you.

💜 I commit to holding space for you in your times of need.

💜 I will let you fly and soar without boundaries.

💜 I will love you through all the ebbs and flows of life, through hardship and ease.

💜 I want you to always be the most authentic version of yourself without judgement and conditions

💜 I will hold space for you to be true to yourself in good times and in bad.

💜 I want you to have your own life, dreams, ambitions, friends, space, and hobbies.

💜 I want us to explore, build, and co-create a life together where we grow.

💜 I trust you with my whole soul and feel safe and secure with you.

💜 I know that you always have my back.

💜 I want an abundant, joyful, prosperous, adventurous life with you.

♥   We know each other's love languages, and we honour them.

♥   We can get through anything together.

♥   I choose you over and over again.

WRITE DOWN WHAT "I LOVE YOU" MEANS TO YOU.

....

....

....

....

....

....

....

....

....

....

....

....

....

....

....

....

....

....

....

LOVE LETTER TO MYSELF – AN EXERCISE IN SELF LOVE

A love letter is a significant and romantic gesture because it's slow, intentional, and deeply personal. Please write a letter to yourself as though it is a letter from your lover. What would you like them to say to you, what words would you want them to use, and how would you like them to communicate with you?

Write the letter and give it to your partner so they can see how you want it communicated.

Here is an example of a love letter.

To my Forever Love

My Dearest Self,

As I sit down to write this letter, my heart swells with admiration and love for the incredible person you are. It's time for you to hear the words that you deserve, to remind you of your worth, and to ignite the fire within you. You are truly a remarkable individual, and it's time you embrace that truth.

From the depths of your soul to the spark in your eyes, there is an undeniable strength that radiates from within you. Your resilience in the face of challenges inspires me beyond words. Life may throw its curveballs, but you have never wavered. Every setback you've encountered has only fuelled your determination to rise above and conquer.

Your dreams and aspirations are a testament to your passion and unwavering spirit. The way you pursue them with unwavering dedication and a hunger for growth is awe-inspiring. Never forget the power you hold to shape your destiny, to create the life you desire. Embrace each opportunity that comes your way, for you are deserving of every success that awaits you.

In times of doubt or uncertainty, remember that you are deserving of love, compassion, and kindness—both from others and from yourself. Take a moment to bask in the beauty of who you are, flaws and all. Embrace your uniqueness and recognize the incredible value you bring to the world. You have the power to make a difference, to touch lives, and to leave a lasting impact.

Believe in your abilities, for you are capable of greatness. Push beyond your comfort zone, for that's where the magic happens. Trust in your intuition and let your dreams guide you forward. Know that you are never alone, for I am always here, supporting you every step of the way.

My love, I am in awe of the person you've become and the person you continue to grow into. You are loved, cherished, and worthy of all the beautiful experiences life has to offer. Embrace your brilliance, embrace your journey, and always remember to love yourself unconditionally.

With boundless love and admiration,

Forever,
Your love

NOW WRITE YOUR LOVE LETTER

....

....

....

....

....

....

....

....

....

....

....

....

....

....

....

....

....

....

....

....

....

CONFLICT MANAGEMENT TECHNIQUES

Every couple will disagree on occasion. The way we navigate these conflicts is of utmost importance in preserving the well-being of the relationship. Employing conflict management strategies in relationships can aid a couple in effectively addressing issues as they surface and fostering a relationship characterized by love, empathy, and personal growth.

Conflict management is the process by which disputes are resolved, where negative results are minimised, and positive results are prioritised. We often see these methods used in the workplace but fail to translate them into the home and marriage, where they can be just as effective.

This key skill involves using different tactics, negotiation, and creative thinking depending on the situation. With properly managed conflict, a marriage is able to minimise interpersonal issues, enhance relationship satisfaction, and produce better outcomes.

Understanding when to apply which style will help you navigate the ebbs and flows of the relationship. Each style having its own pros and cons

1: Accommodating:
This style is about simply putting the other parties needs before one's own. You allow them to 'win' and get their way.

Pros: Small disagreements can be handled quickly and easily, with a minimum of effort.
Cons: Might be viewed as weak if they accommodate too often. Using this technique with larger or more important issues will not solve any issues in a meaningful way and should absolutely be avoided.

2: Avoiding
This style aims to reduce conflict by ignoring it, removing the conflicted parties, or evading it in some manner.

Pros: Giving people time to calm down can solve a surprising number of issues. Time and space can give a much-needed perspective to those in conflict, and some issues will resolve themselves.

Cons: If used in the wrong situations, this technique will make conflicts worse. People can seem incompetent if they overuse avoidance because their partners will think that they are incapable of handling disagreements.

3: Compromising
This style seeks to find the middle ground by asking both parties to concede some aspects of their desires so that a solution can be agreed upon.

Pros: Issues can be resolved quickly, and the parties in conflict will leave understanding more about the other person's perspective. Compromise can set the stage for collaboration down the road and allows both parties to feel heard.

Cons: No one leaves completely happy. In some cases, one side might feel as though they sacrificed too much and be unwilling to compromise again in the future.

4: Compelling
This style rejects compromise and involves not giving in to other viewpoints or wants. One party stands firm in what they think is the correct handling of a situation and does not back down until they get their way.

Pros: People in power using this style show that they are strong and will not back down on their principles. Disputes are solved quickly, as there is no space for any disagreement or discussion.

Cons: People using this style will be seen as unreasonable and authoritarian. Handling conflicts by crushing any dissent will not lead to happy, productive relationships nor to finding the best solutions in most cases.

5: Collaboration
This style produces the best long-term results; at the same time, it is often the most difficult and time-consuming to reach.
Each party's needs and wants are considered, and a win-win solution is found so that everyone leaves satisfied. This often involves all parties sitting down together, discussing the conflict, and negotiating a solution. This is used when it is vital to preserve the relationship between all parties or when the solution itself will have a significant impact.

Pros: Everyone leaves happy. A solution that solves the problems of the conflict is found, and the people who implements this tactic will be seen as skilled.

Cons: This style of conflict management is time-consuming. Relationships can be further broken while solutions are found, which might take a long time, depending on the parties involved and can lead to losses.

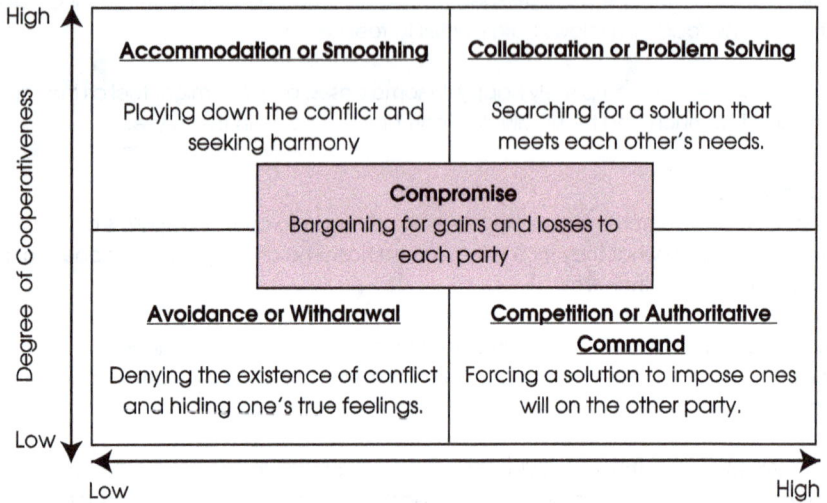

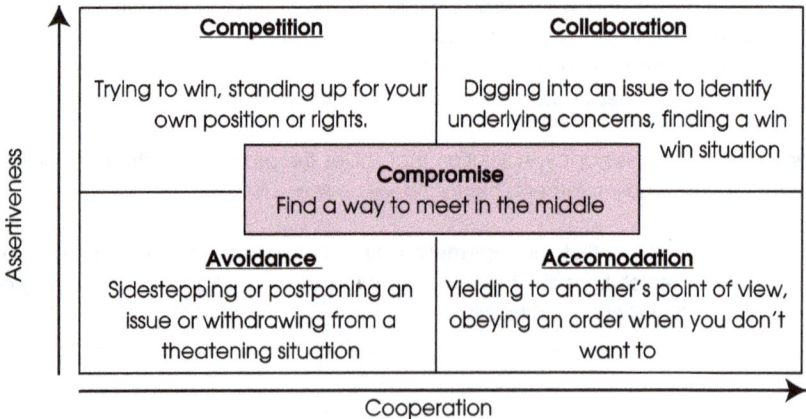

High

Degree of Cooperativeness

Accommodation or Smoothing	Collaboration or Problem Solving
Playing down the conflict and seeking harmony	Searching for a solution that meets each other's needs.

Compromise
Bargaining for gains and losses to each party

Avoidance or Withdrawal	Competition or Authoritative Command
Denying the existence of conflict and hiding one's true feelings.	Forcing a solution to impose ones will on the other party.

Low

Low   High

Assertiveness

Competition	Collaboration
Trying to win, standing up for your own position or rights.	Digging into an issue to identify underlying concerns, finding a win win situation

Compromise
Find a way to meet in the middle

Avoidance	Accomodation
Sidestepping or postponing an issue or withdrawing from a theatening situation	Yielding to another's point of view, obeying an order when you don't want to

Cooperation

8*, 9*

WHAT IS MY CONFLICT MANAGEMENT STYLE?

HOW WILL THIS IMPACT MY RELATIONSHIPS?

ATTACHMENT STYLES

Attachment theory has a long history and has been used as a basis for continuous research. The first step is to get acquainted with the basics and understand the different attachment styles.

According to psychiatrist and psychoanalyst John Bowlby, a person's relationship with their parent's during childhood has an overarching influence on their social, intimate relationships and even relationships at work in the future.

There are four adult attachment styles:

💙 **Anxious** (also referred to as Preoccupied)

💙 **Avoidant** (also referred to as Dismissive)

💙 **Disorganized** (also referred to as Fearful-Avoidant)

💙 **Secure**

Before you start blaming relationship problems on your parents, it is important to note that attachment styles formed during early childhood are *not necessarily identical* to those demonstrated in adult romantic attachments. A great deal of time has elapsed between infancy and adulthood, so intervening experiences also play a large role in adult attachment styles.

Securely attached adults tend to believe that romantic love is enduring. Ambivalently attached adults report falling in love often, while those with avoidant attachment styles describe love as rare and temporary.

While we cannot say that early attachment styles are identical to adult romantic attachment, research has shown that early attachment styles can help predict patterns of behavior in adulthood.

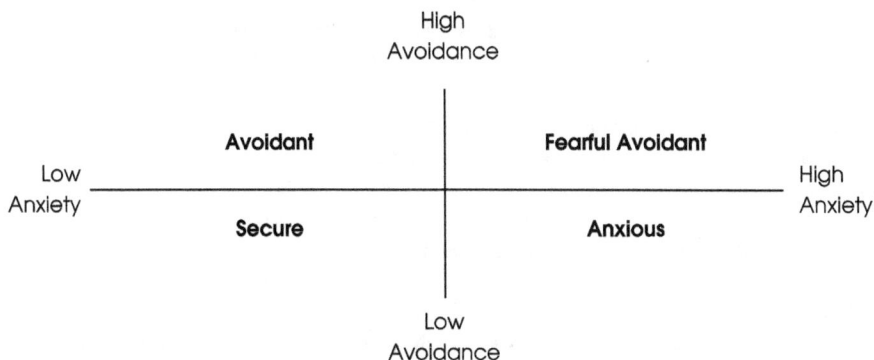

```
                            High
                          Avoidance
                             |
                             |
          Avoidant           |        Fearful Avoidant
Low      _____|_____      High
Anxiety                      |                            Anxiety
          Secure             |           Anxious
                             |
                             |
                            Low
                          Avoidance
```

10*

The Four Attachment Styles:

1: Secure attachment

Secure attachment style refers to forming secure, loving relationships with others. A person with a secure attachment style can trust others and be trusted, love and accept love, and become close to others with relative ease. They're neither afraid of intimacy nor panicked when their partners need time or space away from them. They're able to depend on others without becoming dependent or co-dependent.

2: Anxious attachment (Pre-occupied)

Anxious attachment style is an insecure attachment style marked by a deep fear of abandonment. People with an anxious attachment style tend to be very insecure about their relationships, often worrying that their partner will leave them and thus always needing validation.

Anxious attachment is associated with "neediness" or clingy behaviour in relationships, such as getting very anxious when your partner doesn't text back fast enough and constantly feeling like your partner doesn't care enough about you.

Anxious attachment is also known as anxious-preoccupied attachment, and it generally aligns with the anxious-ambivalent attachment style or anxious-resistant attachment style observed among children.

3: Avoidant attachment (Dismissive)

Avoidant attachment is an insecure attachment style marked by a fear of intimacy. People with an avoidant attachment style tend to have trouble getting close to others or trusting others in relationships because they ultimately don't believe their needs can get met in a relationship.

In relationships, avoidant people typically maintain some distance from their partners or are largely emotionally unavailable. They may even find relationships suffocating and avoid them altogether, preferring to be independent and rely on themselves.

Avoidant attachment is also known as dismissive-avoidant attachment, and it generally aligns with the anxious-avoidant attachment style observed among children.

4: Fearful-avoidant attachment (Disorganised)

Fearful-avoidant attachment style combines both the anxious and avoidant attachment styles. People with fearful-avoidant attachment desperately crave affection and want to avoid it at all costs. They're reluctant to develop a close romantic relationship, yet at the same time, they feel a dire need to feel loved by others.

Fearful-avoidant attachment is also known as disorganised attachment because the attachment behaviours displayed by these individuals can seem inconsistent and oscillate between the extremes of avoidance and anxiousness.

In general, the fearful-avoidant attachment style is relatively rare and not well-researched. But what is known is that this attachment style may be associated with significant psychological and relational risks, including difficulty regulating emotions, heightened sexual behaviour, and increased risk for violence in their relationships.

11*

WHAT IS MY ATTACHMENT STYLE?

....

....

....

....

....

....

....

....

....

....

....

....

....

....

....

....

....

....

....

....

HOW WILL THIS ATTACHMENT STYLE IMPACT MY RELATIONSHIPS?

COMMUNICATION STYLES

Communication styles are patterns of communication and interpersonal behavior that people tend to repeat across different social settings.

THE DISC PERSONALITY ASSESSMENT FRAMEWORK

The DiSC personality assessment framework can help you anticipate how to communicate with your partner in a way that resonates with them.

This model includes four personality types: dominant, influencer, conscientious, and steady. As a bonus, DiSC gives you clues on collaborating best with different people.

Understanding your partner's communication styles is even more critical when you're frequently using video or chat tools.

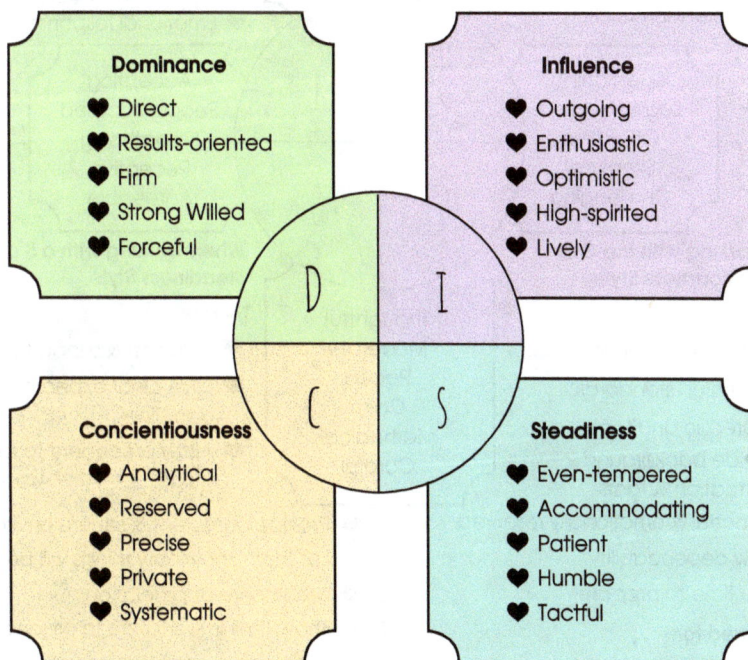

Dominance
- Direct
- Results-oriented
- Firm
- Strong Willed
- Forceful

Influence
- Outgoing
- Enthusiastic
- Optimistic
- High-spirited
- Lively

Concientiousness
- Analytical
- Reserved
- Precise
- Private
- Systematic

Steadiness
- Even-tempered
- Accommodating
- Patient
- Humble
- Tactful

D   I
C   S

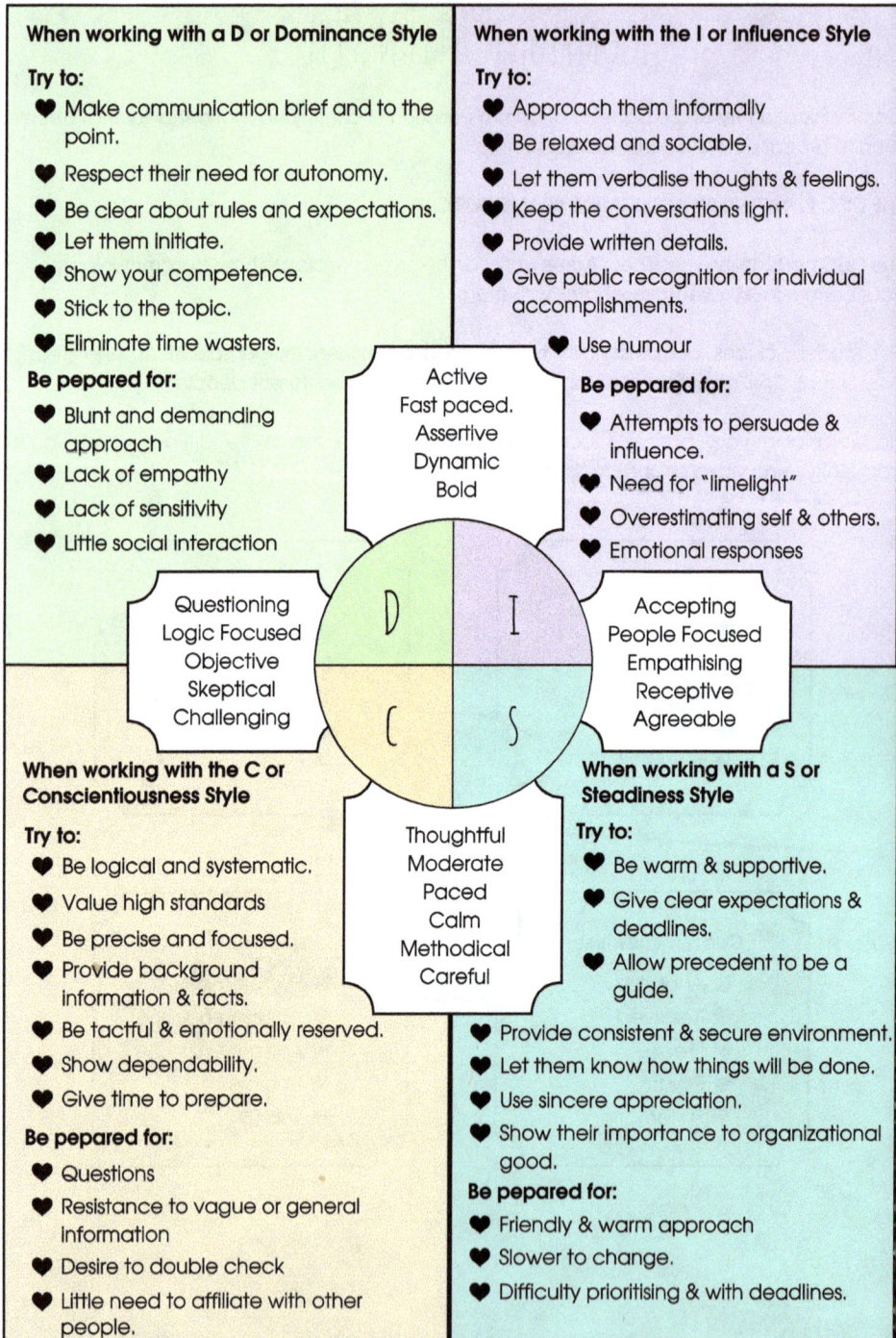

When working with a D or Dominance Style

Try to:
- Make communication brief and to the point.
- Respect their need for autonomy.
- Be clear about rules and expectations.
- Let them initiate.
- Show your competence.
- Stick to the topic.
- Eliminate time wasters.

Be pepared for:
- Blunt and demanding approach
- Lack of empathy
- Lack of sensitivity
- Little social interaction

When working with the I or Influence Style

Try to:
- Approach them informally
- Be relaxed and sociable.
- Let them verbalise thoughts & feelings.
- Keep the conversations light.
- Provide written details.
- Give public recognition for individual accomplishments.
- Use humour

Be pepared for:
- Attempts to persuade & influence.
- Need for "limelight"
- Overestimating self & others.
- Emotional responses

Active
Fast paced.
Assertive
Dynamic
Bold

Questioning
Logic Focused
Objective
Skeptical
Challenging

D

I

Accepting
People Focused
Empathising
Receptive
Agreeable

C

S

Thoughtful
Moderate
Paced
Calm
Methodical
Careful

When working with the C or Conscientiousness Style

Try to:
- Be logical and systematic.
- Value high standards
- Be precise and focused.
- Provide background information & facts.
- Be tactful & emotionally reserved.
- Show dependability.
- Give time to prepare.

Be pepared for:
- Questions
- Resistance to vague or general information
- Desire to double check
- Little need to affiliate with other people.

When working with a S or Steadiness Style

Try to:
- Be warm & supportive.
- Give clear expectations & deadlines.
- Allow precedent to be a guide.
- Provide consistent & secure environment.
- Let them know how things will be done.
- Use sincere appreciation.
- Show their importance to organizational good.

Be pepared for:
- Friendly & warm approach
- Slower to change.
- Difficulty prioritising & with deadlines.

COMMUNICATION STYLES

There are four types of communication styles:

💜 **Passive**

💜 **Passive-Aggressive**

💜 **Aggresive**

💜 **Assertive**

The figure below shows how each communication style can be identified through behaviours.

Table 5 – Identifying Communication Styles

Passive	Passive Aggressive	Aggressive	Assertive
🕙 Emotionally Dishonest 🕙 Indirect 🕙 Inhibited 🕙 Self Denying 🕙 Blaming 🕙 Apologetic	🕙 Emotionally Dishonest 🕙 Indirect 🕙 Inhibited 🕙 Self Denying at first 🕙 Self enhancing at expense of others later.	🕙 Inappropriately honest 🕙 Direct 🕙 Expressive 🕙 Attacking 🕙 Blaming 🕙 Controlling 🕙 Self enhancing at the expense of others.	🕙 Appropriately honest 🕙 Direct 🕙 Expressive 🕙 Self enhancing 🕙 Self confident 🕙 Empathethic to emotions of all involved.
"Others' rights and needs take precedence over mine."	*"I subtly make clear that my rights and needs prevail."*	*"I boldly insist that my rights and needs prevail."*	*"I clearly express that we both have rights and needs."*

The table below shows the actions, looks, beliefs, emotions, and goals of each communication style.

Table 6 - Communication Styles

	Passive	Passive Aggressive	Aggressive	Assertive
Actions	♥ Keeps Quiet. ♥ Puts them-selves down. ♥ Apologises for self-expression. ♥ Hides their dis-agreement. ♥ Inconven-ience them-selves.	♥ Denies personal responsibility. ♥ Covert aggres-sion. ♥ Sarcastic. ♥ Agrees to avoid discussion, then defects on the agreement.	♥ Expresses themselves over others. ♥ Belittle or dismiss others. ♥ Ignores, insults or attacks others' opinions.	♥ Directly express needs, wants and feelings. ♥ Expect others to be equally open and honest. ♥ Accept differ-ent opinions without dismiss-ing them.
Looks	♥ Makes them-selves small. ♥ Looks down. ♥ Avoids eye contact. ♥ Speaks softly.	♥ Like passive.	♥ Makes them-selves large. ♥ Looks threaten-ing. ♥ Penetrating eye contact. ♥ Loud.	♥ Relaxed. ♥ Comfortable body language. ♥ Frequent eye contact (but not glaring)
Beliefs	♥ My needs are less important than others. ♥ I don't have as many rights as others. ♥ My contribu-tions are not as valuable as others.	♥ My needs come first, but I cannot express that openly. ♥ I am not re-sponsible for my actions. ♥ I am entitled to get it my own way, even if I made different commitments.	♥ My needs are more important and justified than others. ♥ I have more rights than others. ♥ My contributions are more valua-ble than others.	♥ My needs are equally impor-tant as others. ♥ I have equal rights. ♥ We both can make valuable contributions. ♥ I am responsible for my behav-iour.

	Passive	Passive Aggressive	Aggressive	Assertive
Emotions	♥ Fear or rejection. ♥ Helplessness. ♥ Low self-esteem. ♥ Frustration. ♥ Resentment towards others who use me.	♥ Fear or rejection if being direct or assertive. ♥ Resentful of people's demands and power. ♥ Fear of being controlled.	♥ Anger. Powerful (or still angry) when winning over others. ♥ Later, potentially remorseful for mistreating others.	♥ Positive feelings about self. ♥ Positive feelings about socializing with others. ♥ Good self-esteem.
Goals	♥ Avoid conflict. ♥ Please others (no matter what the cost to me) ♥ Let others take control (including of my actions)	♥ Get it my way without taking any responsibility. ♥ Get it my way but without having to assert myself.	♥ Win at any cost. ♥ Control others. ♥ Make sure everyone knows who is in charge.	♥ Express themselves. ♥ Find an agreement. ♥ Keep fair boundaries of mutual respect.

Most people tend to adopt a particular communication style's mindsets, values, and beliefs, and those mindsets keep them stuck there.

Knowing your primary communication style and your partner's will help you most appropriately navigate complex communications and conflict.

12*, 13*

WHAT IS MY COMMUNICATION STYLE?

....

....

....

....

....

....

....

....

....

HOW DOES THIS COMMUNICATION STYLE IMPACT MY RELATIONSHIPS?

....

....

....

....

....

....

....

....

....

CRITICAL THINKING

Critical thinking empowers you to present your perspective convincingly and persuasively. It involves the capacity to think in a clear and rational manner, comprehending the logical links between ideas. In essence, critical thinking necessitates the utilization of your knowledge for reasoning. It emphasizes being an engaged learner rather than a passive recipient of information.

Critical thinkers rigorously question ideas and assumptions rather than accepting them at face value. They will always seek to determine whether the opinions, arguments and findings represent the entire picture and are open to finding that they do not.

Critical thinkers will identify, analyse and solve problems systematically rather than by intuition or instinct.

What are the 10 principles of critical thinking?

Principles of Critical Thinking:

- ♥ Gather complete information.

- ♥ Understand and define all terms.

- ♥ Question the methods by which the facts are derived.

- ♥ Question the conclusions.

- ♥ Look for hidden assumptions and biases.

- ♥ Question the source of facts.

- ♥ Don't expect all the answers.

- ♥ Examine the big picture.

If you want to exercise critical thinking skills, ask these questions when you discover new information. These are broad and limitless questions that can be applied across various circumstances.

Table 7 - Critical Thinking Questions

5 WHYS and HOW	Critical Thinking Questions	
WHO	♥ Benefits from this? ♥ Is this harmful to? ♥ Makes decisions about this. ♥ Is most directly affected.	♥ Have you heard also discuss this? ♥ Would be the best person to consult? ♥ Will be the key people in this? ♥ Deserves recognition for this
WHAT	♥ Are the strengths and weaknesses? ♥ Is another perspective? ♥ Is another alternative? ♥ Would be a counter argument?	♥ Is the best- or worst-case scenario? ♥ Is most or least important? ♥ Can we do to make a positive change? ♥ Is getting in the way of our action?
WHERE	♥ Would we see this in the real world? ♥ Are there similar concepts or situations? ♥ Is there the most need for this? ♥ In the world would this be a problem?	♥ Can we get more information? ♥ Do we go for help with this? ♥ Will this idea take us? ♥ Are the areas for improvement?

5 WHYS and HOW	Critical Thinking Questions	
WHEN	♥ Is this acceptable or unacceptable? ♥ Would this benefit our society? ♥ Would this cause a problem? ♥ Is the best time to take action?	♥ Will we know that we have succeeded? ♥ Has this played a part in our history? ♥ Can we expect this to change? ♥ Should we ask for help with this?
WHY	♥ Is this a problem or challenge? ♥ Is it relevant to me or others? ♥ Is this the best or worst scenario? ♥ Are people influenced by this?	♥ Should people know about this? ♥ Has it been this way for so long? ♥ Have we allowed this to happen? ♥ Is there a need for this today?
HOW	♥ Is this like ---(something else)? ♥ Does this disrupt things? ♥ Do we know the truth about this? ♥ Will we approach this safely?	♥ Does this benefit us or others? ♥ Does this harm us or others? ♥ Do we see this in the future? ♥ Do we change this for our good?

14*

PERSONALITY ASSESSMENTS AND MARRIAGE

Marriage between two people is a fantastic and complicated prospect. Each person is different, and nowhere do those differences present themselves more acutely than those who live together and love each other. Our personality types can conflict with those we love, but with better understanding we can communicate and love each other a lot better.

While being different from our spouse isn't bad, conflict can arise if we don't understand where the other person is coming from.

The following personality assessment are my personal preferred assessments. There are many that you can participate in. Choose what is best for you and your spouse.

ENNEAGRAM

The Enneagram provides nine ways of unmasking your false self and improving the marriage. Anytime we experience a breakdown in a relationship or conflict with our spouse, the Enneagram can help us identify how we're complicit in the breakdown. Each of the types has unique "self-destruct" buttons that the false self can't help but press and press and press again. Enneagram personality types can play a role in determining relationship compatibility. Before diving into Enneagram compatibility, it is essential to understand the Enneagram types.

According to the Enneagram Institute, there are nine different Enneagram or personality types, and a scientifically valid test called the RHETI can help people to determine which type best describes their personality. This can go a long way in ensuring better Enneagram relationships.

What are Enneagram relationships?

Enneagram relationships evaluate the compatibility of two people in a relationship, based upon their Enneagram personality types.

Different Enneagram personality types have varying preferences, strengths, and weaknesses and may be more compatible with certain Enneagram types in relationships.

A test that tells you and your partner your Enneagram numbers can help you to determine just how compatible you are. Remember that it is still possible to have a healthy relationship, even if Enneagram types do not appear consistent.

An Enneagram compatibility test is simply a guide that can provide information about what personalities work best together and what can be expected in Enneagram love relationships.

15*, 16*, 17*

ENNEAGRAM TYPES

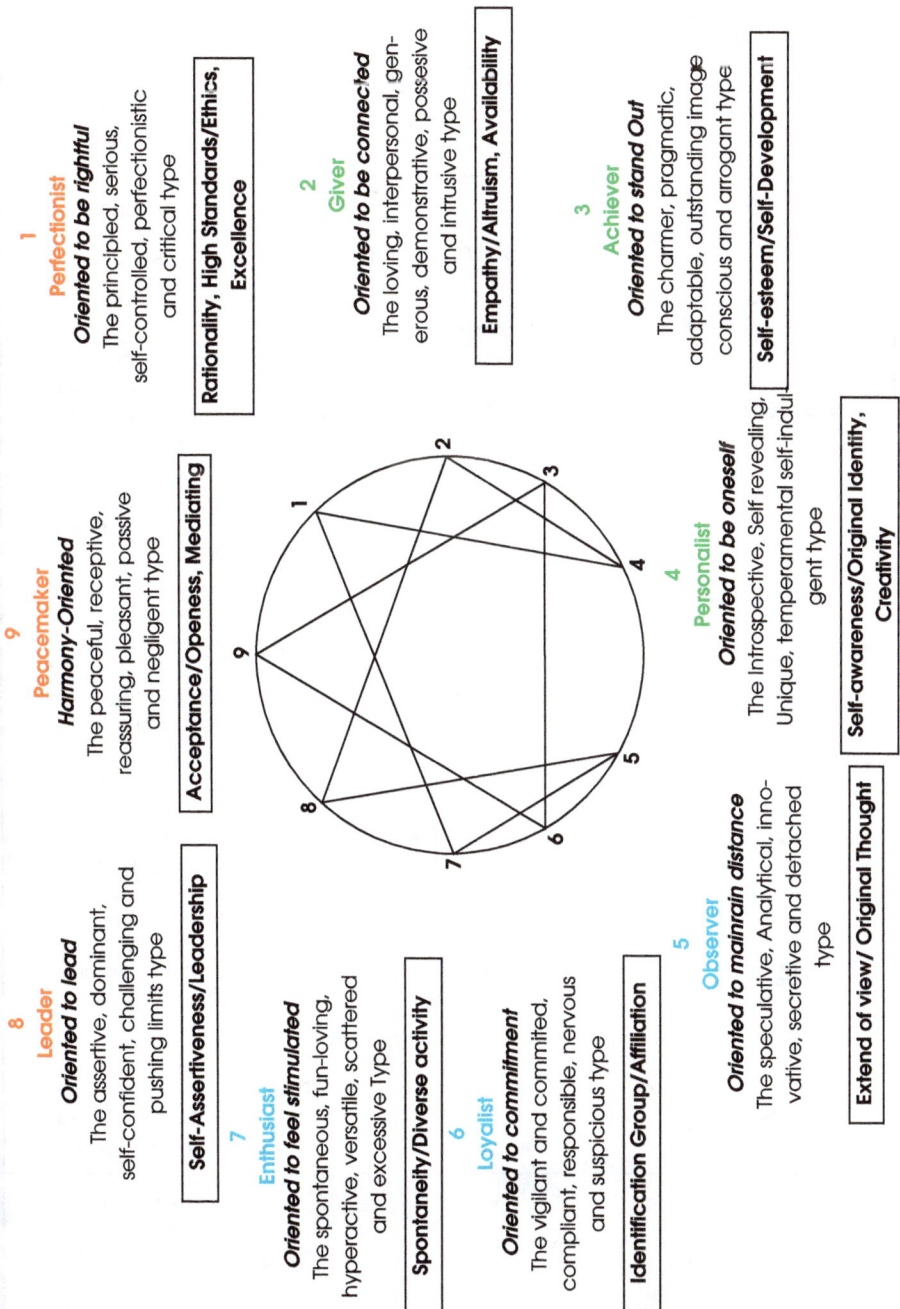

1
Perfectionist
Oriented to be rightful
The principled, serious, self-controlled, perfectionistic and critical type

Rationality, High Standards/Ethics, Excellence

2
Giver
Oriented to be connected
The loving, interpersonal, generous, demonstrative, possessive and intrusive type

Empathy/Altruism, Availability

3
Achiever
Oriented to stand Out
The charmer, pragmatic, adaptable, outstanding image conscious and arrogant type

Self-esteem/Self-Development

9
Peacemaker
Harmony-Oriented
The peaceful, receptive, reassuring, pleasant, passive and negligent type

Acceptance/Openess, Mediating

4
Personalist
Oriented to be oneself
The Introspective, Self revealing, Unique, temperamental self-indulgent type

Self-awareness/Original Identity, Creativity

8
Leader
Oriented to lead
The assertive, dominant, self-confident, challenging and pushing limits type

Self-Assertiveness/Leadership

7
Enthusiast
Oriented to feel stimulated
The spontaneous, fun-loving, hyperactive, versatile, scattered and excessive Type

Spontaneity/Diverse activity

6
Loyalist
Oriented to commitment
The vigilant and committed, compliant, responsible, nervous and suspicious type

Identification Group/Affiliation

5
Observer
Oriented to maintain distance
The speculative, Analytical, innovative, secretive and detached type

Extend of view/ Original Thought

Table 8: Enneagram Types

#	Enneagram Type	Characteristics	Description
1	Perfectionist	Rationality, High Standards/ Ethics, Excellence	Oriented to be rightful. The principles, serious, self-controlled, perfectionistic, and critical type.
2	Giver	Empathy/Altruism, Availability	Oriented to be connected. The loving, interpersonal, generous, demonstrative, possessive and intrusive type.
3	Achiever	Self-Esteem/Self Development	Oriented to stand out. The charmer, pragmatic, adaptable, outstanding image conscious, and arrogant type.
4	Personalist	Self-awareness/Original Identity, Creativity	Oriented to be oneself. The introspective, self-revealing, unique, temperamental, self-indulgent type.
5	Observer	Extent of view/Original Thought	Oriented to maintain distance. The speculative, analytical, innovative, secretive, and detached type.
6	Loyalist	Identification Group/Affiliation	Oriented to commitment. The vigilant and committed, compliant, responsible, nervous, and suspicious type.
7	Enthusiast	Spontaneity/Diverse activity	Oriented to feel stimulated. The spontaneous, fun loving, hyperactive, versatile, scattered, and excessive type.
8	Leader	Self-assertive/Leadership	Oriented to Lead. The assertive, self-confident, dominant, challenging and pushing limits type.
9	Peacemaker	Acceptance/Openness, Mediating	Harmony oriented The peaceful, receptive, reassuring, pleasant, passive, and negligent type.

MYERS BRIGGS

The Myers-Briggs Personality Type Indicator is a self-report inventory designed to identify a person's personality type, strengths, and preferences. Isabel Myers and her mother, Katherine Briggs, developed the questionnaire based on their work with Carl Jung's theory of personality types. Today, the MBTI inventory is one of the world's most widely used psychological instruments.

The Myers-Briggs Type Indicator (MBTI)—also referred to as the "Myers-Briggs personality test" or simply the "Myers-Briggs test"—is a self-reported questionnaire. The test helps people assess their personality using four specific dichotomies or scales: introversion-extraversion, sensing-intuition, thinking-feeling, and judging-perceiving.
Within the four areas of the MBTI personality test, possible conflicts may arise when couples have opposing traits.

- ♥ **Introvert vs. Extrovert**
- ♥ **Sensing-Intuiting**
- ♥ **Thinking/Feeling**
- ♥ **Judging/Perceiving**

ENFJ, INFJ, ESFJ, ISFJ
- ♥ Meets spouse's needs first.
- ♥ Will "check in" throughout the day.
- ♥ Is positive to keep spouse happier.
- ♥ Offers thanks in ways they like to be shown thanks.

ENFP, INFP, ESFP, ISFP
- ♥ Is patient with spouse.
- ♥ Respects spouse's unique identity.
- ♥ Gives spouse space/alone time.
- ♥ Offers strong loyalty.

ENTJ, INTJ, ESTJ, ISTJ
- ♥ Always loyal.
- ♥ Ventures to understand spouse.
- ♥ Beams with pride over spouse.
- ♥ Offers protection.

ENTP, INTP, ESTP, ISTP

💜   Offers honesty.

💜   Sets the bar high and reaches for it.

💜   Protects spouse.

💜   Offers no judgment, no matter what.

What's Your Personality Type?

Use the questions to determine the four letters of your Myers-Briggs Type.

For each pair of letters, choose the side that seems the most natural to you, even if you don't agree with the description.

Table 9: MBTI Questions

Are you outwardly or inwardly focused		How do you prefer to make decisions?	
♥ Could be described as talkative, outgoing. ♥ Like to be in a fast-paced environment. ♥ Tend to work out ideas with others, think out loud. ♥ Enjoy being the center of attention.	♥ Could be described as reserved, private. ♥ Prefer a slower pace with time for contemplation. ♥ Tend to think things through inside your head. ♥ Would rather observe than be center of attention.	♥ Make decisions in an impersonal way, using logical reasoning. ♥ Value justice, fairness. ♥ Enjoy finding the flaws in an argument. ♥ Could be described as reasonable, level-headed.	♥ Base your decision on personal values and how your actions affect others. ♥ Value harmony, forgiveness. ♥ Like to please others and point out the best in people. ♥ Could be described as warm, and empathetic.
E **Extraversion**	**I** **Introversion**	**T** **Thinking**	**F** **Feeling**
How do you prefer to take in information?		How do you prefer to live your outer life?	
♥ Focus on the reality of how things are. ♥ Pay attention to concrete facts and details. ♥ Prefer ideas that have practical applications. ♥ Like to describe things in a specific, literal way.	♥ Imagine the possibilities of how things could be. ♥ Notice the big picture and how everything connects. ♥ Enjoy ideas and concepts for their own sake. ♥ Like to describe things in a figurative, poetic way.	♥ Prefer to have matters settled. ♥ Think rules and deadlines should be respected. ♥ Prefer to have detailed step-by-step instructions. ♥ Make plans, wants to know what you are getting into.	♥ Prefer to leave options open. ♥ See rules and deadlines as flexible. ♥ Like to improvise and make things up as you go. ♥ Are spontaneous, enjoy surprises and new situations
S **Sensing**	**N** **Initiation**	**J** **Judging**	**P** **Perceiving**

ISTJ	ISFJ	ISFJ	INTJ
Responsible, sincere, analytical, reserved, realistic, systematic. Hardworking and trustworthy with sound practical judgement.	Warm. Considerate, gentle, responsible, pragmatic, thorough. Devoted caretakers who enjoy being helpful.	Idealistic, organised, insightful, dependable, compassionate, gentle, seek harmony, and cooperation, enjoy intellectual stimulation.	Innovative, independent, strategic, logical, reserved, insightful. Driven by their own original ideas to achieve improvements.
ISTP	**ISFP**	**INFP**	**INTP**
Action-oriented, logical, analytical, spontaneous, reserved, independent. Enjoy adventure, skilled at understanding how mechanical things work.	Gentle, sensitive, nurturing, helpful, flexible, realistic. Seek to create a personal environment that is both beautiful and practical.	Sensitive, creative, idealistic, perceptive, caring, loyal. Value inner harmony and personal growth, focus on dreams and possibilities.	Intellectual, logical, precise, reserved, flexible, imaginative. Original thinkers who enjoy speculation and creative problem solving.
ESTP	**ESFP**	**ENFP**	**ENTP**
Outgoing, realistic, action-oriented, curious, versatile, spontaneous. Pragmatic problem solvers and skillfull negotiators.	Playful, enthusiastic, friendly, spontaneous, tactful, flexible. Have strong common sense, enjoy helping people in tangible ways	lEnthusiastic, creative, spontaneous, optimisitic, supportive, playful. Value inspiration, enjoy starting new projects, sees potential in others.	Inventive, enthusiastic, strategic, enterprising, inquisitive, versatile. Enjoy new ideas and challenges, value inspiration.
ESTJ	**ESFJ**	**ENFJ**	**ENTJ**
Efficient, outgoing, analytical, systematic, dependable, realistic. Like to run the show and get things done in an orderly fashion.	Friendly, outgoing, reliable, conscientious, organised, practical. Seek to be helpful and please others. Enjoy being active and productive.	Caring, enthusiastic, idealistic, organised, diplomatic, responsible. Skilled communicators, who value connection with people.	Strategic, logical, efficient, outgoing, ambitious, independent. Effective organisers of people and long range planners.

18*, 19*

INSIGHTS PERSONALITY

At the very start of the self-awareness journey is Insights Discovery. A psychometric tool based on the psychology of Carl Jung, Insights Discovery is built to help people understand themselves, understand others, and make the most of the relationships that affect them in the workplace.

The Insights Discovery methodology uses a simple and memorable four-colour model to help people understand their style, strengths, and value they bring to the team. We call these the colour energies, and it's the unique mix of Fiery Red, Sunshine Yellow, Earth Green and Cool Blue energies, which determines how and why people behave the way they do.

Insights Colours and Personalities

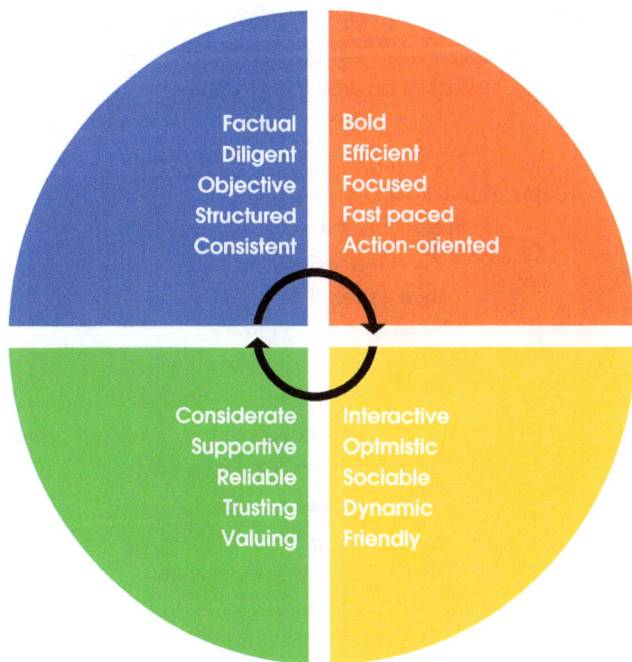

Factual	Bold
Diligent	Efficient
Objective	Focused
Structured	Fast paced
Consistent	Action-oriented
Considerate	Interactive
Supportive	Optimistic
Reliable	Sociable
Trusting	Dynamic
Valuing	Friendly

LIFE

I find beauty in things others never see.
I find hope there too.
Life is what you make it.
Life is taking not so beautiful things and making them beautiful.
It is finding hope even when there is none.
This is not an easy thing to do but
I find that love is the answer to most things, if not all things.
Why mot love more?
If you do not give your love away, then it means nothing.
In essence, it is wasted love.
No one will ever feel it.
Love is meant to be felt.
To be given away freely,
Regardless of what you get back in return.
We all want our lives to have meaning.
So, we can say we were here, and we loved with everything that we had.
My life is not perfect, but it is mine and
I never wanted perfect.
I want real. I want to feel.
And, I have loved, really loved. A lot.
And, above all I have lived really lived.
And God, I still love.

~ N.R. HART

THE TOP 10 REASONS FOR DIVORCE IN SOUTH AFRICA

According to records of 500 divorce actions instituted in South Africa during 2011, the reasons below were most cited on why couples divorced. If we understand the grounds for divorce, we can work on these items before marriage and during our marriage with self-awareness and empathy to ensure successful, enduring relationships.

10. Difference in Priorities

9. Religious Differences

8. Parental Responsibilities

7. Finances

6. Sexual Incompatibility

5. Addiction

4. Social media

3. Marriage Infidelity

2. Psychological, Physical, Financial or Emotional Abuse

1. Lack of Communication

Delving deeply into questions and answers around your views on the above areas of your marriage, before and during the marriage, will help you manage the conflicts in your relationships as you navigate the relationship fully aware.

20*

CHAPTER FOUR:
RELATIONSHIP ASSESSMENT
DATE NIGHTS WITH YOUR PARTNER

"After a while, you just want to be with the one that makes you laugh."
—Chris Noth as Mr. Big, Sex and the City

DATE NIGHT QUESTIONS

These questions to ask your spouse are only suggestions. You can come up with hundreds more on your own. Don't stop with these. Use these questions regularly and approach conversations with your spouse differently.

There are so many fun things for couples to discuss beyond just the daily life routine.Commit to never stop learning about your spouse.

Every day is a new opportunity to learn something new, to connect in a new way and see your spouse in a new and exciting light!

- What would you collect if you could start a collection, and money was not an option?
- What is the accomplishment you are most proud of?
- What is your favourite day of the week and why?
- What was your favourite toy growing up?
- What is your favourite childhood memory?
- Who would you like to meet that has passed away?
- What is your greatest fear?
- What would you do if it were you last day on earth? How would you spend it?
- If you were to die today, what would be your biggest regrets?
- What would you say your gifts are?
- What would you say is your purpose on Earth?
- What was your favourite tradition growing up as a kid?
- Who would you give it to if you had a million dollars to give away?
- If you had a million dollars to spend on your family, how would you spend it?
- If you could be on a T.V. game show, what would it be?

What superpower would you choose to have?

What is your biggest pet peeve?

What do you hope you will be remembered for after you die?

Describe your perfect day.

What skill would you want to learn if money or time weren't an issue?

When do you feel most alive?

If you could relive one year, which would it be?

Do you rely most on your head or heart when you make decisions?

What has been your biggest disappointment or failure in life?

What is your favourite memory of the two of us?

What attracted you to me when we first met?

What is your most embarrassing moment?

What would they be if the house were to catch fire and you could only grab (3) things?

If you had to choose between the Internet or A.C./Heat, which would you choose?

Do you have any fetishes? What are they?

What is the most daring thing you have ever done?

What is the most significant risk you have ever taken?

What is your favourite article of clothing and why?

Would you instead cook or clean? Why?

When do you feel most alive?

What was your favourite Halloween costume growing up?

Who was your first crush?

Who is your celebrity crush?

What was the first concert you ever went to?

Do you remember the first movie you saw in the movie theatre?

What is the strangest food you have ever tried?

What is your least favourite thing to eat?

If you could pick one house chore NEVER to have to do again, what would it be?

What is your favourite place that you have visited?

What would it be if you could eat only 1 thing for the rest of your life?

What would be the title if your Life were a book?

If your life were made into a movie, what celebrity would you want to play you?

If you were to write a song about the year 2020, what would be the title?

What was the best and worst thing that you experienced during the pandemic?

What adventure do you dream of going on?

What do you like best about our relationship?

If you could relive one day, what would it be?

If you were an animal, what would you be and why?

Do you prefer snail mail or email and why?

What is the most unique gift you have ever received?

What is the worst gift you have ever been given?

In what way are you most like your mom?

In what way are you most like your dad?

What is your favourite thing that I do for you?

What is one quality you are grateful you didn't receive from your parents?

Where would you go if you could travel anywhere in the world?

If you could work for a charity, which would you choose and why?

Have you ever been stuck in an elevator?

Can you imagine a time when you were the most scared?

If your car had a name, what would it be?

If you could go back and live in a different period, what would it be and why?

Would you rather skydive or bungee jump and why?

What is the best date we have ever been on?

What age would you like to stay forever?

What would you do if you could spend 24 hours alone?

What grosses you out? What are your "icks"?

Have you ever gotten into trouble with the cops?

What is the worst nightmare that you have ever had?

Who is the worst boss you ever had?

- What was the worst job you ever had?
- What has been your favourite job?
- If money wasn't an option, what kind of car would you buy?
- If a genie could grant you (3) wishes, what would they be?
- What is your favourite song?
- Describe yourself in 5 words,
- If you had to get a tattoo today, what would it be and where?
- What do you think is the most important quality is for friendship?
- What do you think is our best couple quality?
- If you could learn a foreign language, which one would you choose?
- If you could spend the day with a celebrity, who would it be?
- What do you want to see for our family in five years and in ten years?
- What do you feel is your strongest character trait?
- What is your favourite book that you have read?
- What is your favourite movie?
- What would it be if you could learn to play an instrument?
- Do you have a funny fart story?
- What is your favourite place/space in our home?
- What quality of yours do you hope our children get?
- What is the hardest lesson you have ever had to learn?
- Where was your first kiss and with who?
- What is your worst habit?
- What are (3) things that bring you joy?
- What do you wish you were better at?
- What is your biggest weakness?
- What is your favourite time of day?
- If you could own any animal as a pet, which one would you choose?
- If you could have dinner with a person in the religious texts other than God, who would it be?
- If you could have a second home, what would it be like and where would it be?
- If you had a choice between seeing or hearing, which would you choose and why?

21*

FUN GAMES AND PERSONALITY TESTS/QUIZZES

❤ Play the **"Never Have I Ever"** game with your future spouse to find out things about your spouse in a fun way.

❤ Play **"30 Seconds"** with your future spouse to test their general knowledge to open conversation areas.

❤ Play **"Monopoly"** to test financial understanding and decision making.

❤ Take love language quizzes to learn each other's love languages.

❤ Enneagram test and coaching – how to work with the other enneagrams to ensure conflict management, effective communication, and how to grow together as a couple.

15*, 16*, 17*, 18*

THE RELATIONSHIP ASSESSMENT:
QUESTIONS TO ASK YOUR FUTURE SPOUSE BEFORE MARRIAGE

These questions are meant to stimulate discussions between the couple. There is no right or wrong answer. It is recommended that you answer each relevant question to the best of your ability.

The answers are meant to be discussion points and may highlight potential areas of dispute and conflict that may arise in the future.

This is your opportunity to discuss your responses and find acceptable strategies to deal with them before they arise, or to manage any potential future risk by means of a prenuptial contract or marriage counselling.

Have open and honest discussions and debates about these questions and answers so that you can strengthen your relationship bonds.

Remember, you can disagree and still love each other.

💛 **MARRIAGE CONTRACT QUESTIONS**

The Marriage Contract Questions will guide you to understand how to structure your marriage contract. It will be helpful to research your country's Marital Regimes and Laws and use that information to create a sound pre-nuptial agreement.

- What is your concept of marriage?
- Have you ever been married before?
- Are you married now?
- What are your expectations of marriage?
- What is your general definition of success?
- How would you define a successful marriage?
- How do we decide which marital regime will be best for us?
- Do you have any assets or inheritance that must be excluded from the contract?
- Do you have anything else that requires exclusions in the marriage contract?
- Do you want to get married COP, ANC with accrual and ANC without accrual, and why?
- Do you intend to start a business now or in the future?
- What if I stop working and we sign an ANC without accrual? How will I be protected in the event of a divorce?

- Do you also want to get married religiously?
- What are the conditions under which you will want a divorce? What are non-negotiables?
- If we have children, what are your views on parenting post-divorce and maintenance payments towards a spouse and children?
- How would you manage conflicts and disputes arising during our marriage?
- How do you feel about dowries? How much dowry will you accept or give?

❤ THE WEDDING

Often wedding planning and execution are much cause for stress, with some marriages not taking place because the couple did not have meaningful conversations around the wedding.

These questions will highlight potential areas of conflict that can arise from planning a wedding and handled prior so you can enjoy your wedding day.

- How much money should we spend on the wedding?
- How will the costs of the wedding be split?
- Can we get financial support for the wedding?
- How much influence will your family have on the wedding?
- What will you do if our family starts dictating what should happen at our wedding?
- How do you feel about wedding planners?
- How many guests will we have?
- How important is the menu to you?
- What types of food will we have?
- What décor will we have?
- How do you feel about destination weddings?
- Will the wedding be traditional or modern?
- What will you wear for the wedding?
- What gifts would you like for the wedding?
- How do you feel about wedding vows?
- How do you feel about wedding ring designs? Would you want to design your ring?
- How will we communicate disagreements about the guests?
- How do you feel about bachelor or bachelorette parties?

🕐 When will these parties take place before the wedding? What is off-limits?

🕐 How many celebrations will take place for the wedding, over how many days?

🕐 Do you believe that we should go on a honeymoon?

🕐 Where will we go for the honeymoon?

🕐 Do we need a budget for the honeymoon?

🕐 If we were to be gifted the honeymoon, would that be a problem?

🕐 Do you want bridesmaids and groomsmen, and who will they be?

🕐 Do we need specific seating arrangements at the wedding, and why?

❤ DREAMS/BUCKET LIST GOALS

A successful marriage goes beyond the wedding day. Couples need to have marriage goals along with personal goals. This section deals with a discussion of your short-, medium- and long-term goals.

Look at these questions, the Marriage SWOT analysis, and the Marriage Strategic Plans section to guide you.

🕐 What are your goals in life?

🕐 Identify three things that you want to accomplish short-term.

🕐 Identify three things that you want to achieve medium term.

🕐 Identify three things that you want to accomplish, long-term.

❤ CHARACTER TRAITS

Characteristics and Values are essential in your spouse. It is helpful to articulate and elaborate on what the priority characteristics and values are in your future spouse. Look at this section and the Characteristics of your Spouse section to guide you.

🕐 Why have you chosen me as your potential spouse?

🕐 What are the most important characteristics that you look for in your spouse?

🕐 What are the values that you would like in your spouse?

🕐 How important are looks and physical characteristics to you in your spouse?

🕐 Are you a spiritual person?

🕐 What is the role of religion in your life?

🕐 What is your understanding of traditional marriage (state the relevant religion)?

🕐 What are you expecting of your spouse, religiously?

- What is the role of a husband?

- What is the role of a wife?

- Do you have an addictive personality?

- Have you ever cheated on a past partner?

- Are you temperamental or easily angered?

- Would you say that you were a jealous person?

- Why did your past relationships fail?

- If I were to ask your best friend to describe you, what would they say?

- If I were to ask your worst enemy to describe you, what would they say?

♥ CUSTOMARY MARRIAGES

You may note your specific religious or customary marriage questions here. I have mentioned Muslim marriages as an example.

- What is your understanding of Muslim Marriage?

- What is your understanding of the spouse's rights in Islamic Marriage?

- What are your views on initiating divorce?

- Can I get a clause in the marriage contract to exercise my right to Talaaq (Muslim Divorce) should I no longer be wished to be married?

- Under what circumstances can I exercise my right to Talaaq (Muslim Divorce)?

- Do you want to practice polygamy? Would you ever want a second wife? If so, how would we approach this? Discuss whether a second wife is an option.

- What is the relationship between yourself and the Muslim community in your area?

- Are you volunteering in any Islamic activities?

♥ FAITH AND SPIRITUALITY

Faith and spirituality are not always linked to religion but may cause conflict and disputes when the couple is not aligned with their belief system. These questions will get you talking about areas of spirituality and faith to help manage any conflict that may arise.

- What are your spiritual or religious beliefs?

- What can you offer your spouse spiritually?

- How important is it for you to keep a spiritual or religious practice? Which practices are most important to you?

🕉 How would you feel about your spouse wanting to change their religion later?

🕉 How often do you practice your faith, and how often do you expect me to?

🕉 How do you feel about religious holidays, and how, where and with whom do you think they should be celebrated?

🕉 How involved are you in your spiritual or religious community?

🕉 How much do you expect me to be involved in your spiritual or religious activities?

🕉 Do you expect our children to be raised with a particular spiritual or religious faith?

🕉 Do you expect our children to go through certain religious rituals?

❤️ **FAMILY RELATIONSHIPS**

When a person marries, they often marry into a family, not just the individual. Family relationships are a huge cause of conflict and disputes. Some of these questions will start the discussion around the complexity of moving from being single to becoming a cohesive family unit.

🕉 What is your relationship like with your parents, sisters, and brothers?

🕉 Describe how your family have reacted to any past relationships that you have had and why?

🕉 How emotionally and financially dependent is your family on you?

🕉 What is your relationship with your extended family?

🕉 How was your parent's relationship with each other?

🕉 What do you expect your relationship to be like with the family of your spouse?

🕉 What do you expect the relationship between your spouse and your family to be like?

🕉 Is there anyone in your family that lives with you now?

🕉 What happens if someone from my family needs to live with us?

🕉 What happens when someone from the family wants to borrow money?

🕉 Are you planning to have anyone in your family live with you in the future?

🕉 What should be done if my relationship with your family turns sour?

🕉 Are there any divorces in your immediate family?

🕉 Do you plan to live near your parents or move near them as they age?

🕉 How do you feel about my family? Why?

🕉 Who is your favourite and least favourite family member on my side and your side, and why?

🕉 How often are we going to visit or receive visits from our families?

- How do you expect to spend the holidays?
- Who sits in the car's front seat with you while driving? Will this change after our marriage?
- What is your opinion of speaking other languages in the home that I do not understand? With friends? With family?
- How do you feel about blended families?

♥ FRIENDS

Friendships will change post-marriage. When you bring another person into your life, you will also introduce them to your friends. If you want to sustain friendships, you will need to have discussions around friends' compatibility.

- Who are your friends? Identify at least three.
- Are your friends married or in relationships?
- How did you get to know them?
- Why are they your friends?
- What do you like most about them?
- What do you like least about them?
- What will your relationship with them be like after marriage?
- Do you have friends from the opposite sex?
- What is the level of your relationship with them?
- What will be the level of your relationship with them after marriage?
- What relationship do you want your spouse to have with your friends?
- How often will you be going out with your friends?
- Do your friends drink alcohol, take drugs or gamble?
- Would I need to ask permission to go out with my friends?

♥ ENTERTAINMENT

Entertainment can be various things and can vary across culture, race and religion. Defining and articulating what is fun for you is essential as these areas when left uncommunicated, may result in issues later.

- What are the things that you do in your free time?
- What is your favourite movie and why?
- What is your favourite song and why?

- What is your favourite colour and why?
- Who is your favourite actor and singer, and why?
- Do you have boys'/girls' nights and weekends? What do you do in this time?
- Do you go to strip clubs?
- Have you ever been with a prostitute?
- Have you ever done drugs? Are you still doing drugs?
- Do you gamble?
- Do you have an addictive personality?
- Do you smoke? How much and how often?
- Do you drink alcohol? How much and how often?
- Do you like to have guests in your home for entertainment?
- What are you expecting from your spouse when your friends come to the house?
- How often will guests be coming over to the house?
- Who will cook? Will the food be catered?
- Who will clean after guests leave? Will there be help from a maid?
- How often do you post on social media?
- Which social media platforms are you on?
- How many followers do you have on each platform?
- How do you feel about placing our children's pictures on social media?
- How do you feel about me putting sexy pictures on social media?
- How do you feel about exes on social media following you?
- How would you feel about me smoking or drinking in our shared space?

♥ VACATIONS and TRAVEL

Couples need a break too. However, sometimes vacations can add to the stress you are trying to escape by going on vacation. These questions can help you plan how you go on holiday better.

- Do you travel? How often?
- What is your view on spending money on vacations, e.g., do you like to stay in expensive hotels or have any requirements on which class airline we travel?
- Do you travel for work or holidays?
- Where is your favourite destination in the world, and why?

- How do you spend your vacations?
- Who will pay for vacations?
- How often do you like to travel with your family and friends?
- Will we travel together as a couple?
- How do you think your spouse should spend vacations?
- What do you love about travelling?
- What don't you love about travelling?
- If we were to lose our passport travelling, have an incident whilst travelling, or get lost in an unknown place, how would you react to that, and why?

❤ **SELF CARE**

How you care for yourself is essential. You cannot pour from an empty cup. Questions on self-care will reveal how much time and attention your partner places on themselves and can also show how to support each other here. This section could also link i.t.o. Love Languages.

- Do you believe in self-development?
- Where are you in your journey of self-development?
- Do you read books?
- What do you read, and how often?
- What is your favourite book and why?
- Who is your favourite author, and why?
- Do you exercise?
- What exercise do you do? How often?
- Do you compete in sports?
- Do you have a problem with me exercising at a public gym?
- How do you feel about me having a personal trainer?
- Do you have hobbies? What are they, and how often do you participate in them?
- Do you wax, shave, laser or do anything like spa days?
- How do you feel about aesthetic improvements? i.e., Botox, plastic surgery, orthodontics
- Are there any self-care practices you would want me to participate in?
- Do you see a therapist or a healer? How often?
- How do you feel about alternate holistic therapies?

❤ LOVE LANGUAGE

Knowing each other's love language will remove a lot of conflict from the relationship. Look at the section on Love Languages to understand what your and your partner's love languages are so that you can cater to them.

🕘 What is your love language?

🕘 How would you like me to express my love in your love language?

🕘 Do you think that you are one to express romantic feelings verbally?

🕘 Do you think that you want to express affection in public?

🕘 How do you express your admiration for someone that you know – now?

🕘 How do you feel about saying – "I Love You."

🕘 What does "I Love You" mean to you?

🕘 How often does it need to be said?

🕘 How much time do you think we need to spend with each other?

🕘 How much alone time do you need?

❤ CONFLICT MANAGEMENT

Knowing your conflict management style will create awareness when conflict arises. You will have more empathy with this awareness and help each other manage conflict better.

🕘 What is your conflict style — avoidant, accommodating, compromising, or something else?

🕘 How did your family deal with conflict growing up?

🕘 How do you usually express anger?

🕘 How comfortable are you with having arguments or disagreements?

🕘 What do you think our perpetual conflicts are (those based on personality or lifestyle differences)?

🕘 What part of me is most annoying to you?

🕘 What would be an example of a resolvable conflict in our relationship?

🕘 Can you imagine an example of a conflict you felt we dealt with successfully?

🕘 What would be unacceptable to you in a disagreement?

🕘 How do you express your feelings to someone who has done a favour for you?

🕘 Do you like to write about your feelings or journal?

- If someone has wronged you, how do you want them to apologise to you?

- If you wrong someone, how do you apologise?

- How do you feel about someone not apologising if they don't think they wronged you?

- How much time passes before you choose to forgive someone?

- How do you make important and less important decisions in your life?

- Do you use foul language at home? In public? With your family?

- Do your friends use foul language?

- Does your family use foul language?

- How do you express anger?

- How do you expect your spouse to express anger?

- What do you do when you are angry? Are you emotionally avoidant, aggressive, violent or can you speak about an issue and resolve the conflict amicably?

- When do you think initiating mediation or counselling in a marriage is appropriate?

- How should the conflict be resolved when there is a religious dispute in your marriage?

- Define mental, verbal, emotional, and physical abuse. What is your understanding of this?

- Has there been any history of abuse in your family or with you?

- What would you do if you felt that you had been abused?

- Who would you call for assistance if you were being abused?

- How would you feel if we were watching a series together and I went ahead and watched the rest of it without you one day? How would you communicate these feelings?

- How would you feel about me entering T.V. shows, Competitions or Pageants?

- How would you feel about me studying further?

- Do you believe we can disagree and still love each other?

❤ HEALTH

"In sickness and in health" has been well used in wedding vows, but how many of us endure marriages through health issues? Knowing health issues upfront and working through them together can help you have a long, happy marriage, and the awareness can help you plan your health requirements together as a couple.

🕙   Do you suffer from any chronic disease or condition?

🕙   Are you willing to take a physical exam by a physician before marriage?

🕙   What is your understanding of proper health and nutrition?

🕙   How do you support your health and nutrition?

🕙   How do you feel about mental health and mental fitness?

🕙   Is there a history of mental illness in the family? How was it handled?

🕙   Do you have any mental illnesses?

🕙   How would you feel if I developed a physical or mental illness in our relationship? Would you stay?

🕙   Are there any chronic illnesses in your family?

🕙   Do you have medical aid? What plan are you on?

🕙   Are there any reservations about how medical aid should be spent?

🕙   What are your views on vaccines and vaccinations?

🕙   What are your views on homoeopathic and alternative healing?

❤ FINANCES

One of the highest conflict areas in marriages is finances. It is imperative to have open, honest, transparent discussions around finances as a couple to ensure that when this conflict arises that it is dealt with proactively and intelligently.

🕙   What is your definition of wealth?

🕙   How much money do you make?

🕙   What is more important, money or love?

🕙   What assets do you currently have?

🕙   Who will buy the assets in our marriage and why?

🕙   Whose name will the assets be in?

🕙   What inheritances do you have?

🕙   Would you say you have a lack or abundance mentality, and why do you say this?

- If you have a "lack mentality", how does that surface in a relationship?

- How were your parents spending growing up?

- How was money viewed in your family? Is it something to be enjoyed or a necessary evil?

- What was your family's attitude towards money, and how do they resemble to yours?

- Do you have a will and investments? Who are the beneficiaries? Will this change when we are married? How often do you update your Will? Who is the Will with?

- How do you feel about joint accounts?

- If we buy property, will it be in our names or just one?

- How will we take up business ventures together?

- Are we allowed to go into business with family and friends?

- How much debt do you have (student loans, credit card, mortgage) if any?

- How comfortable are you borrowing money?

- What are your ideas on other people borrowing money from us?

- Are we going to make it a priority to save money together?

- Do we sign a pre-nuptial agreement before we get married? If so, what will it cover? Should we get divorced, how will we go about it? Mediation, Shared Attorney? How will we split assets and liabilities?

- Do you agree to consult with me about any significant expense ahead of time, even if you are planning to use your own money?

- Are you comfortable creating a budget for our married life together?

- How are we going to share the expenses after we get married?

- If you have an ex or children from previous marriages, what are your financial obligations to them?

- Do you have any other financial obligations to another person, whether for legal or moral reasons, that I should know about?

- What is important to you financially — owning a house, a nice car, expensive clothing, travelling?

- What is more critical for you, the size of a house or its location?

- Do you plan to buy or rent?

- How important is contributing to charity to you, and which charities are your favourites?

- Who is going to pay the bills?

- If we split bills, how will they be split and why?

- Who will pay for the holidays?

- How will we split the costs of the household?

- What am I expected to pay for? What will I need to pay for with regards to the children?

- Do you currently use a budget to manage your finances?

- How do you spend your money?

- How do you save your money?

- How do you think that your use of money will change after marriage?

- Do you have any debts now? If so, how are you making progress toward eliminating the debt?

- Do you use credit cards?

- What is your credit score?

- Do you support taking loans to buy a home and/or car?

- What are you expecting from your spouse financially?

- What is your financial responsibility in a marriage?

- Do you support the idea of a working wife?

- If so, how do you think a dual-income family should manage funds?

- Who are the people to whom you are financially responsible? How will this change when we are married?

- How would you feel if I earned more than you?

♥ CHILDREN

Kahlil Gibran says that "Our children are not our children; they are the sons and daughters of life's longing for itself. Many of us may disagree with the philosophy from "The Prophet" and many other ways to raise children. These questions may highlight those areas where you agree and perhaps where you don't. These questions can help you craft a parenting strategy if you choose to have children.

- Do you want to have children? If not, why?

- How many children would you like?

- When do you want to start trying?

- Do you have preferred names for our children? Where do they originate from, and what does it mean to you?

- Can your family dictate how we raise our children? What influence will your family have over how we raise our children?

- What if we agree either not to have or to have children, and I change my mind?
- What are the three most important values you are planning to teach our children?
- What kind of parenting approach are you planning to implement?
- Why do you think the child needs to be breastfed or bottle-fed?
- When we start having children, how do you envision your share of responsibilities?
- What is your perspective on having one of us be a stay-at-home parent?
- Do you have children now?
- What is your relationship with your children now?
- What is your relationship with their parent now?
- If you or I have children from a previous relationship, how do you envision our blended family?
- If you have kids from a previous relationship, what role are you willing to take, or would you like me to take with the stepchildren?
- What is a mother's role to the children?
- What is the father's role?
- Do you support utilising babysitters, maids, and other helpers?
- To the best of your understanding, are you able to have children?
- Do you believe in abortion in your family?
- If there are any unique medical conditions with the children, how will we handle that?
- What relationship do you expect your spouse to have with your children and their parent?
- What is the best method of raising children?
- What kind of discipline is appropriate or not appropriate?
- What is the best method of disciplining children?
- How were you raised?
- How were you disciplined?
- Do you believe in spanking children? Under what circumstances?
- If your child said that they were homosexual, how would you handle that?
- Do you believe in public or private schools for your children? Why?
- Do you believe in religious schools for your children?
- Do you believe in home-schooling your children? If so, by whom?

What relationship should you children have with other religions/races, classmates, and friends?

Would you send your children to visit their extended family if they lived in another province, state, or country?

What relationship do you want your children to have with all their grandparents?

How would we communicate conflict when the children are around?

Are the children allowed to have sleepovers? Why or why not?

Who are the children allowed to go on holiday with?

Do we allow children to have mobile devices and access to the internet?

How would you manage internet safety for the children?

Are you particular about the type of diet that the children should follow?

How do you feel about buying gifts for the children?

What involvement will our families have when raising our children?
How often are the children expected to visit the families?

If there are members of my family that are of a different culture or race, what type of relationship do you want to have with them?

How would you split contact and care with the children if we divorced? What would the expectation be?

How will we maintain the children?

If both of us were to die whilst the children were still minor, who would the children go to live with and be raised by?

Who will be allocated guardianship of the children?

If the baby has a congenital disability in the womb, would you want to have the baby or abort and why?

How do you feel about adoption?

How do you feel about adopting children from a different race to you or me?

How would you feel if your child opened about being LGBTQ to you? How would you react?

♥ **PETS**

Pets are often like our children. Some people love them, some dislike them, and some are indifferent, but no doubt they will need to be discussed when getting married.

- How do you feel about pets?
- Do you have any pets, or have you had any pets in the past?
- What pets would you like us to have?
- Are pets allowed in the house/ on the bed?
- Do you have any pet allergies?
- If we were to relocate, would you take the pets with us?
- How do you feel about our pets being on medical aid?
- What is your favourite animal and why?
- Should we get divorced, and who gets to keep the pets? How will we share contact with the pets?

♥ **INTIMACY**

While a fulfilling sex life is essential to a healthy relationship, intimacy extends beyond sex. Being in sync when it comes to physical pleasure and understanding what each of you needs to meet your emotional needs will bring you closer, whereas a lack of communication in this area will surely tear you apart. (For couples that have chosen to abstain from sex before marriage, these questions may need to be asked after marriage.)

- What are your expectations regarding sex?
- How often are you expecting sex?
- If you are not getting sex as much as expected, how will you communicate this to me?
- Who must initiate sex?
- How would you like me to initiate sex?
- How do you feel about foreplay? Is it necessary for you?
- What is your idea of foreplay?
- What is essential around sex hygiene for you?
- How open are you to telling me if you are not satisfied sexually?
- What do you enjoy most about sex?
- Do you have any kinks?
- How do you feel about having sex when the woman is on her period?

- How do you feel about oral sex?
- Do you consume pornography, and if so, how do you feel about it?
- What turns you on most about me?
- Have you ever had doubts about your sexuality?
- Do you think I am physically affectionate enough in our relationship?
- Is there anything off-limits sexually?
- What are your fantasies?
- Do you agree to bring up any attraction you feel outside of our relationship before something significant develops? How would you like this conversation to take place?
- If we are having issues with our sex life, how would you like to address it?

❤️ **RELATIONSHIPS AND COMMITMENT**

Commitment in a relationship provides a sense of security and control. It is vital to be on the same wavelength as what a committed relationship entails.

- How do you feel about fairy tales?
- What was the perfect example of a relationship that you saw growing up?
- Do you want to know about my past relationships and why?
- What time did you feel most connected and loved in our relationship?
- What is the most important daily task that you will need help with?
- How can we consciously decide to tell each other if we feel we're being taken for granted?
- What does our commitment mean to you?
- What is the most romantic thing we have done together, and why?
- Why do you want to be married, and why do you want to be married to me?
- What are the three things you most appreciate about me?
- What are the three things you most admire about me?
- What first attracted you to me?
- Can you explain what chemistry and connection mean and what creates harmony and chemistry with you?
- How do you envision our life in five years? In 10? In 20?
- What do you love about me that you hope never changes?
- What do you think you will have to give up when we get married or move in together?

97

- Is there anything you want me to change or give up after we get married?
- What kind of partner do you aspire to be?
- Do you need some time alone, and if so, how often?
- Are you willing to schedule one evening a week to regularly sit down with each other and catch up about our relationship goals and challenges?
- How often will we have date nights?
- What support do you expect from me in challenging times (illness, death, unemployment), and what does that support look like?
- What is your definition of infidelity?
- Is cheating forgivable?
- If someone hits on me while I'm out or at work, should I tell you?"
- If someone flirts with you, will you tell me?
- How do you feel about polygamy, open relationships, and polyamory?

❤ COMMUNICATION

Communication in a relationship is like oxygen to life; without it, it dies. Poor communication is the leading cause of conflict and breakdown in marriages. It is essential to know your communication style. This awareness alone will change the way you communicate. Refer to the section on Communication Styles to help you navigate some of the questions below.

- What is your communication style?
- What would be your preferred method of communication during a conflict?
- How comfortable are you with me sharing my feelings, even if they are negative?
- Would you consider yourself emotionally intelligent?
- What is your understanding of the difference between IQ and EQ?
- How do you feel when I disagree with you?
- What are your political/religious beliefs?
- How do you feel about lies?
- Would you tell me a white lie to avoid hurting my feelings?
- What's the worst white lie anyone has told you?
- Is there something in how I say things when I'm angry that makes you feel criticised?
- What would you say is nagging to you?
- Do you think I nag?

🕐 How would you expect me to react if I catch you telling lies?

🕐 Can I look at your phone at any time?

🕐 Will you provide me with access to your passwords?

🕐 What causes you to become disappointed, embarrassed, or ashamed?

🕐 Have I ever disappointed you or caused you pain?

🕐 How will you communicate with me if I invoke those feelings?

🕐 Have we discussed and resolved those times, or are they still affecting our relationship?

🕐 Is there anything about me that attracts you now but might annoy you over the years?

♥ **WORK AND CAREER**

Today's most significant issues in marriages involve each spouse's career. Work is a major part of everyone's life, and balancing work and career needs can be challenging while maintaining a healthy, happy marriage. Couples often find themselves in conflict over the jobs of one or both spouses. Even though it is a lot of work, balancing your career and marriage is possible.

🕐 What are your career goals in both the near and distant future?

🕐 How do you feel about working after hours and weekends?

🕐 What is your understanding of work-life balance?

🕐 What is your understanding of work-life integration?

🕐 How many hours do you spend at work now?

🕐 If I get offered my dream job in another part of the country, would you be willing to move with me?

🕐 Are you okay with me quitting my job to care for our children?

🕐 What are your expectations of me as a spouse or parent when working?

🕐 How will I be protected if we are married Out of Community of Property and we get divorced? Will you pay Spousal and child maintenance?

🕐 What if I can't stand my work situation and need a break? Will you support me leaving work?

🕐 How would you feel if I worked long hours for extended periods?

🕐 How are your relationships with your work colleagues?

🕐 Who do you like working with the most and why?

🕐 Who do you like working with the least, and why?

🔄　What is most important to you at work?

🔄　If you could choose money or job satisfaction, which would you choose and why?

🔄　How do you feel about me earning more than you do?

🔄　How open are you to listening to my day at work?

🔄　How do you feel about both of us working remotely at home?

❤️ **LIFESTYLE PREFERENCES**

One of the critical decisions a couple needs to make in a marriage is lifestyle. Ultimately, a lifestyle represents a set of choices driven by underlying values.

🔄　What does your ideal day off look like?

🔄　What does your ideal vacation look like?

🔄　Do you have hygiene standards?

🔄　How do you feel about my cleanliness and neatness standards?

🔄　How will we divide the chores?

🔄　Are you okay with hiring help to clean?

🔄　Who will do the shopping and cooking in our relationship?

🔄　Do you have any dietary requirements?

🔄　What if I don't have the exact dietary requirements as you? Will that be an issue?

🔄　How often do you plan to eat out?

🔄　What kind of restaurants do you enjoy most?

🔄　How important is it for you to eat at the dinner table without T.V. or electronic distractions?

🔄　How do you feel about the T.V. in the bedroom?

🔄　Hobbies will change as we change. For example, how will this affect our relationship if I take up Golf when married and spend weekends playing golf? How will you feel about changing hobbies, and how do we manage this?

🔄　Do you snore?

🔄　How do you feel about me sleeping in another room because of sleeping habits that impact us negatively?

🔄　How do you feel about LGBTQ and same-sex relationships?

22*; 23*

40 RULES OF LOVE

RULE 40

A life without love is of no account.

Don't ask yourself what kind of love you should seek,

spiritual or material, divine or mundane, Eastern or Western.

Divisions only lead to more divisions.

Love has no labels, no definitions.

It is what it is, pure and simple.

Love is the water of life.

And a lover is a soul of fire!

The universe turns differently when fire loves water.

~ELIF SHAFAK

CHAPTER FIVE:
"JOYOUSLY, EVER AFTER"
MARRIAGE ADVICE

"There are a hundred paths through the world that are easier than loving. But who wants easier?" —Marry Oliver

Marriage advice is often given just before marriage when the couple is in the throes of planning the wedding and is very much in love. The advice is only sometimes heard and lived. It is essential to sit down and take some time to consider marriage advice from married people and people who have been married. You can learn as much from failures as you can from success stories.

Here are some wisdom snippets of marriage advice collected from different sources and personal experiences.

- Never lose your sense of self in the pursuit of pleasing people.

- Compromise everything except yourself.

- Be independent and invest in your self-growth.

- Have your group of friends aside from mutual friends.

- Two wholes make a whole. You are a complete individual. You do not complete each other, but you can help co-create a life together and heal together if required.

- Look after yourself like you did when you met. Self-Care is important.

- You do now OWN each other. You are two separate individuals and should continue to remain as such.

- Know how to listen and be present with and for your partner.

- Choose someone with the same or similar values and life philosophies as you.

- Marriage is a partnership where you need to work on supporting each other.

- Never compare your marriage to anyone else

- Make your own rules that help you make your marriage work.

- Don't sweat the small stuff.

- Work together as a team to resolve issues. It is not you against them; it is the both of you against the problem.

- Understand your partner deeply and intuitively and know what turns them on and off, mind, body, and soul.

♥ Don't make assumptions.

♥ Sometimes doing nothing together is fantastic. Enjoy those moments.

♥ Accept that your partner is human and fallible and makes mistakes. Work through them

♥ Walk, talk, hold hands, and go on dates.

♥ Trust each other, be open, and be honest.

WRITE DOWN ANY OTHER MARRIAGE ADVICE THAT YOU FIND USEFUL

....

....

....

....

....

....

....

....

....

....

....

....

....

....

....

CHOICES

Marriage is hard. Divorce is hard.

Choose your hard

Obesity is hard. Being fit is hard.

Choose your hard.

Being in debt is hard. Being financially disciplined is hard.

Choose your hard.

Communication is hard. Not communications is hard.

Choose your hard.

Life will never be easy. It will always be hard.

But we choose our hard.

Pick wisely.

~UNKNOWN

MARRIAGE AS A STRATEGY
HOW TO USE SWOT TO IMPROVE YOUR MARRIAGE

"Love is like a friendship caught on fire."
—Bruce Lee

WHAT IS SWOT?

SWOT stands for strengths, weaknesses, opportunities and threats, and the SWOT model is used in most businesses as a framework to create a strategy. This framework, when applied to relationships such as marriage, a business partnership, friendship and more, help solidify and improve the associations based on awareness to grow positively.

HOW TO USE S.W.O.T. TO ASSESS YOUR MARRIAGE.

Follow the steps below with your spouse, and answer honestly. When you share weaknesses, it is wise to share YOUR weaknesses in the marriage and let your spouse share theirs.

You can help each other counter weaknesses with your strengths to bring balance and equilibrium to the marriage.

Strengths are internal, positive attributes of your marriage. You and your spouse can build upon these within your control to strengthen a strong marriage.

Examples of Strengths that can be looked at:

Goals, conversation, problem-solving style, conflict management style, communication style, careers, skills, hobbies, friends, interests, finances, parenting style, and love language.

They can be articulated as follows:

Spiritual worldview, desire for personal growth, ability to use humour in conflict, goal oriented and focused, personal growth focused, entertaining; conversation; abundance mindset; parenting philosophy, enneagram-type positive attributes.

PINPOINT YOUR WEAKNESSES

Weaknesses are negative factors that detract from or weaken the marriage. The weaknesses that each person brings to the marriage must first be recognised and then improved.

Here are some questions to help each person discover weaknesses they bring to the relationship.

Examples of Weaknesses that can be looked at:

- Health condition
- A financial issue
- Aging parents
- Family conflict
- Gruelling work schedule
- Personality traits
- Mental health issues
- Addictions
- Past relationships
- Communication and conflict styles
- Religious differences
- Different thoughts on money and parenting

They can be articulated as follows:

- Driven by career.
- Hyper independence
- Temperamental and easily angered.
- Avoidant, disorganised attachment style,
- Passive aggressive communication styles
- Love languages are not known.
- Jealous and possessive
- Family triggers

FIND OPPORTUNITIES TO BECOME BETTER

Opportunities are external factors in your marriage that can make the relationship better or stronger.

Examples:

❤️ Companionship

❤️ Emotional support

❤️ Family building

❤️ Financial partnership

❤️ Personal growth

❤️ Shared goals

❤️ Intimacy and romance

❤️ Support system

❤️ Friendship and social interactions

❤️ Community and social connections

❤️ Cultural exchange

FIND POTENTIAL THREATS IN THE MARRIAGE

Threats are external factors that can tear your marriage down or break it apart. Recognising the threats will help us all protect your marriages and set boundaries in place.

Examples:

❤️ Communication problems

❤️ Separate friend groups, individual pursuits, separate spending habits

❤️ Secretive behaviour

❤️ Online risks include pornography, conversing with old flames on social media

❤️ A financial crisis, health crisis, another man/woman

❤️ Unsupported independent pursuits, not travelling, and letting busyness and distraction make me susceptible to outside temptation

USE SWOT IN ANY OTHER IMPORTANT RELATIONSHIP

This SWOT analysis can be applied to any significant relationship. Simply follow the process and adapt it to the specific relationship you're involved in. Whether it's parenthood, a business partnership, a friendship, or any other connection, most aspects of life come with challenges, but it's up to you to decide which challenges you're willing to embrace.

24*

EXAMPLE OF A SWOT ANALYSIS

	STRENGTHS	**WEAKNESSES**
INTERNAL (RELATED TO THE PERSON)	e.g. ❤ Academic ❤ Great Cook ❤ Adventurous ❤ Funny ❤ Healthy ❤ Goal Orientated Achiever ❤ Financial stability ❤ Honest, Transparent and Ethical	❤ Anxious and insecure attachment style ❤ Family triggers ❤ Divorce Trauma ❤ Fertility issues ❤ Jealous ❤ Competitive
	OPPORTUNITIES	**THREATS**
EXTERNAL (RELATED TO THE ENVIRONMENT)	❤ Build a business together. ❤ Travel ❤ Philanthropic and Charitable work	❤ Social Media ❤ Economic downturn

CREATE YOUR SWOT

	STRENGTHS	WEAKNESSES
INTERNAL (RELATED TO THE PERSON)		
	OPPORTUNITIES	THREATS
EXTERNAL (RELATED TO THE ENVIRONMENT)		

VERBALISE YOUR PLAN OF ACTION.

A visual plan should articulate marriage goals for the short, medium, and long term. You may have a joint swot for your marriage and your individual goals.

Once you use SWOT to assess your marriage in all four areas, verbalise to one another your action plan. Each of you will speak out loud to the other specific ways YOU will change or contribute to improving the marriage. Verbalising these makes them more accurate and writing them solidifies them even more.

Remembering that life does not always go according to plan is essential. The plan needs to be fluid and adjustable with life's curve balls. Be flexible and kind with these plans. Whilst planning is essential, do not forget to enjoy the joys of being present and living in the NOW.

EXAMPLE: OUR MARRIAGE GOALS

Short Term (1-5 years)	Medium Term (5 – 10 years)	Long Term (10 years to Joyously Ever After)
Buy a home	Pay off bond	Build and run a business
Travel to Europe	Have children	Travel the world
Charity work – giving back	Travel to the 7 wonders of the world	Financial freedom
Study further to improve skills	Healthy lifestyle	Philanthropic work
Have fun	Have fun	Have fun

WRITE DOWN YOUR MARRIAGE GOALS BASED ON YOUR SWOT

Short Term (1-5 years)	Medium Term (5 – 10 years)	Long Term (10 years to Joyously Ever After)

MARRIAGE KEY PERFORMANCE INDICATORS (KPI'S) AND METRICS

WHAT ARE KPI'S AND METRICS?

Key Performance Indicators (KPIs) and metrics are tools used in various fields to measure and evaluate the performance, progress, and effectiveness of an organization, project, or individual. While they are related concepts, they have distinct characteristics. KPIs are a subset of metrics. KPIs are strategic, high-level indicators chosen to assess progress toward specific objectives, while metrics encompass a broader range of data points, including those that may not be tied to key strategic goals.

Table 8: Difference between KPI's and Metrics

KPI'S	METRICS
Measure progress towards goals.	Measure the performance of specific activities or processes
High-Level Perspective	Lower-Level Perspective
Used for Strategic Decision Making (i.e., How is the marriage performing? Do we need to adjust the goals)	Tend to be more day-to-day operational or tactical activities.

Questions that you can ask to define KPI's and Metrics.

💜   What is your definition of success?

💜   What does your "rich life" look like? What is wealth to you? (Money, health, freedom etc.)

💜   What criteria will you employ to gauge the prosperity of your marriage?

💜   How will you keep track and evaluate them?

You can choose to record them on a spreadsheet or display them on a chalkboard in plain view. Use whatever method suits your preferences.

Although I acknowledge that numerous facets of marriage involve abstract emotions and are challenging to quantify, even these aspects can be assessed to some extent.

Marriage Metrics can be:

♥ Communication effectiveness: This can be measured through the frequency and quality of communication between spouses.

♥ Conflict resolution: The ability to resolve conflicts healthily and constructively.

♥ Emotional intimacy: The level of emotional connection and closeness between spouses.

♥ Commitment level: The level of commitment and dedication to the relationship.

Examples of Tangible, Measurable KPI's can be:

♥ Number of Date Nights in a month or year, or the

♥ Number of Family Vacations taken

♥ Activities that we do together.

♥ Business or career goals supported, pursued and achieved.

♥ Hobbies that we do together, hobbies that we do apart

♥ Family or friends' entertainment functions per month etc.

WRITE DOWN YOUR MARRIAGE METRICS AND KPI'S BASED ON YOUR MARRIAGE GOALS

OUR KPI'S	OUR METRICS

DRINK TO ME ONLY WITH THINE EYES

Drink to me only with thine eyes,

And I will pledge with mine;

Or leave a kiss but in the cup

And I'll not look for wine.

The thirst that from the soul doth rise

Doth ask a drink divine;

But might I of Jove's nectar sup,

I would not change for thine.

I sent thee late a rosy wreath,

Not so much honouring thee

As giving it a hope that there.

It could not withered be;

But thou thereon didst only breathe,

And sent'st it back to me;

Since when it grows, and smells, I swear,

Not of itself but thee!

~Ben Johnson

MY MARRIAGE VOWS

A vow is a solemn promise to do a specified thing or dedication to someone or something. Your wedding vows should represent your commitment to each other as a couple and your relationship. Wedding vows typically share heartfelt expressions of love and loyalty promises to loftier ideals.

Take your time when writing them so they are meaningful and articulate what this commitment means to you.

If you need to get your mind working around the articulation of vows, here are some examples of Wedding Vows

- ❤ You are my lover and my teacher,

- ❤ You are my model and my accomplice, and you are my true counterpart.

- ❤ I will love you, hold you, and honour you,

- ❤ I will respect you, encourage you and cherish you, in health and sickness, through sorrow and success, for all the days of my life.

- ❤ I promise to be your biggest fan.

- ❤ I will always encourage your growth.

- ❤ I promise to work with you to heal and grow.

- ❤ I want to be someone you can "sit in the mud" with when things are not going well.

- ❤ I promise to be an active listener and help when you need help, but I give you the space you need when you need that.

- ❤ I promise to be always honest and transparent.

- ❤ Nothing is off-limits for discussion.

- ❤ I promise never to ask you to be something you are not.

- ❤ I will try to be calm when you are angry.

- ❤ I commit to accepting that you live without boundaries, Wild and Free

- ❤ I will always allow you to Dream and Just Be authentically you.

- ❤ I commit to adopting a win-win mindset where I work toward outcomes from current and future disagreements to get what is best for us as a couple.

- ❤ I vow to have the patience that love demands, to speak when words are needed, and to share in the silence when they are not.

♥ I love your sense of adventure and how you always brighten my day.

♥ I vow to join you in this journey as your wife/husband with an open heart and to make even the smallest of our accomplishments—eating breakfast or changing a light bulb—into an exciting part of our lives together."

♥ They say love is like magic, and I couldn't agree more. When I first met you, you seemed to appear out of nowhere. I focused on you, consistently trying to solve the puzzle of who you were and where you were from. As our love grew, I couldn't wait to see you again and be entertained by our chemistry. I look forward to unlocking the world's mysteries with you as we wed.

WRITE DOWN YOUR MARRIAGE VOWS

MARRIAGE PRINCIPLES

Marriage principles can guide couples to establish a good foundation for their marriage. And these can help you get through tough times as a couple.

You probably already know that marriage is indeed hard work if you are already married. And as a couple who is new to marriage, you may want to create principles by which to navigate your married life.

The Five Agreements are a beautifully simplified way to assist couples in navigating through any hardships that may come.

THE FIVE AGREEMENTS - Don Miguel Ruiz

According to Don Miguel Ruiz, in his book on the Five Agreements, everything we do is based on agreements we have made — agreements with ourselves, with other. people, with God, and with life.

But the most important agreements are the ones we make with ourselves. With these agreements, we tell ourselves who we are, how to behave, what is possible, what is impossible.

The Four Agreements slowly help you to recover your authentic self and the real you start to awaken.

With The Fifth Agreement comes the complete acceptance of yourself just the way you are, and the complete acceptance of everybody else just the way they are. The reward is your eternal happiness. The Fifth Agreement is made with words, of course, but its meaning and intent is beyond the words. The Fifth Agreement is ultimately about seeing your whole reality with the eyes of truth, without words.

BE IMPECCABLE WITH YOUR WORD

Speak with integrity. Say only what you mean. Avoid using the word to speak against yourself or to gossip about others. Use the power of your word in the direction of truth and love.

DON'T TAKE ANYTHING PERSONALLY

Nothing others do is because of you. What others say and do is a projection of their own reality, their own dream. When you are immune to the opinions and actions of others, you won't be the victim of needless suffering.

DON'T MAKE ASSUMPTIONS

Find the courage to ask questions and to express what you really want. Communicate with others as clearly as you can to avoid misunderstandings, sadness, and drama. With just this one agreement, you can completely transform your life.

ALWAYS DO YOUR BEST

Your best is going to change from moment to moment; it will be different when you are tired as opposed to well rested. Under any circumstance, simply do your best, and you will avoid self-judgment, self-abuse, and regret.

BE SKEPTICAL, BUT LEARN TO LISTEN

Don't believe yourself or anybody else. Use the power of doubt to question everything you hear: Is it really the truth? Listen to the intent behind the words, and you will understand the real message.

25*

WRITE DOWN YOUR MARRIAGE PRINCIPLES

....

....

....

....

....

....

....

....

....

....

....

....

....

....

....

....

....

....

....

....

....

....

OUR MARRIAGE MANIFESTO

What do I commit to doing in our marriage?

A manifesto is a published declaration of the intentions, motives, or views of the issuer.

Your marriage manifesto focuses more on your values as expressed through your behaviour within your relationship and will inspire your relationship to exist and grow with purpose and direction.

Explore and decide how you will bring your best self forward in your relationship, no matter what situations or challenges arise.

You can turn your marriage manifesto into an artwork that can be displayed as a reminder of the values you choose to live by as a couple.

Our Marriage Manifesto

WE WILL ASSUME **THE GOOD** AND DOUBT THE BAD | We will pour LOVE into pain
WE WILL SHOW GRACE TO EACH OTHER

We will come out of tough times STRONGER than when we went in | We will keep the SEX going

Forgive Quickly ♥ Kiss Slowly ♥ Laugh Heartily

We will always be BEST FRIENDS & **LOVERS** ⟶ | We will write our own unique love story

We will face problems as a team

LOVE is an ACTION, not just a FEELING

WE BELIEVE IN NEW DAYS, FRESH STARTS AND DO OVERS

WE WILL BE A CHAMPION FOR EACH OTHER IN ALL THINGS | We will choose to LOVE each other even in the moments when we struggle to like each other

WE CHOOSE TO KEEP IT FIGHT FOR IT WORK FOR IT

We will hold fast to each other, cuddle, flirt and hold hands

Wherever we are, when we're together we are home!

WRITE DOWN YOUR MARRIAGE MANIFESTO

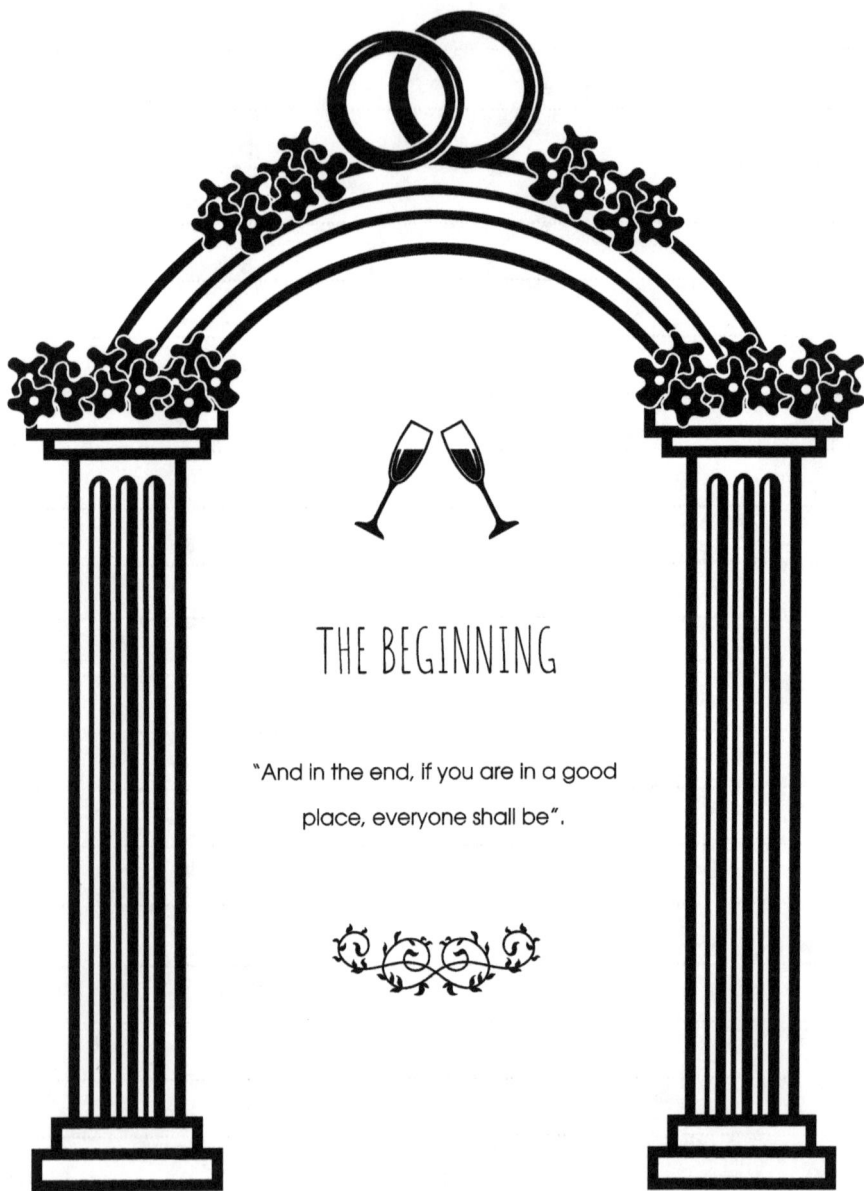

THE BEGINNING

"And in the end, if you are in a good place, everyone shall be".

ABOUT THE AUTHOR

Shubnum is an internationally accredited Family Law Mediator and I.T Executive from South Africa.

She has been through many highly litigated cases in her own contested Divorce.

Had she known the benefits of Mediation and been aware of mediation practices upfront, her experiences may have differed.

Mediating divorces and pre-marital mediation have given Shubnum a world of knowledge and information on how to ensure that conflict is managed within a marriage, so that it does not lead to a divorce.

Through the alchemy of turning pain into power, she believes that living a life of service is where true purpose lies. She hopes this planner brings structure and clarity in times of uncertainty.

With her degrees in Information Technology, Investment and Corporate Finance and a Master of Business Administration, she opted to pursue a career in Family Law Mediation to help couples part peacefully and amicably. She graduated as Valedictorian of her Family Law Mediation studies.

Now she wants to take that a step further and assist couples in planning their Marriages so that it does not end in Divorce. Using the frameworks for building a successful business strategy, she has adapted these concepts to building a successful marriage beyond the wedding day.

She believes planning your Marriage allows you to think about the process.

Information is an asset, and knowledge is power. Having a plan allows you to make informed decisions, create self-awareness, and enhance your love for each other, which leads to growth as a couple, reinforcing the knot as it is meant to be.

Here's to living

🕊 *Joyously, Ever After* 🕊

ACKNOWLEDGEMENTS

I would like to express my extreme gratitude to the many individuals who have played a significant role in the creation and completion of this book. Without their support, encouragement, and contributions, this project would not have been possible.

First and foremost, I want to thank my family for their unwavering love and support throughout this journey, especially my little girl who has been my inspiration for everything that I do. I love you very much. Your belief in me and constant encouragement drove my determination to see this book come to life.

I am immensely grateful to my friends, whose enthusiasm and motivation kept me going during moments of doubt and fatigue. Your words of encouragement and constructive feedback were invaluable in shaping the final manuscript.

To the entire publishing team, from Print on Demand, thank you for your expertise, guidance, and meticulous attention to detail. Your dedication and commitment to producing a high-quality book are deeply appreciated. To Carlen Human from Identity Designs for her creative artistry in the design of the book.

I am indebted to the experts and individuals who generously shared their knowledge and experiences, lending credibility and depth to the content. Your insights and expertise enriched this book, and I am honoured to have had the opportunity to learn from you.

I extend my gratitude to the readers who will embark on this literary journey with me. Your curiosity and willingness to explore new ideas are what inspire authors to continue writing.

To those of you who are embarking on the adventure or marriage, I wish you love, peace, contentment and lasting joy on your journey.

Lastly, I want to express my heartfelt appreciation to all those who have touched my life in ways big and small. Your kindness, support, and belief in my abilities have been instrumental in shaping both my personal and writing journeys.

Writing this book has been a transformative experience, and I am humbled and grateful for the collective efforts that have brought it to fruition. Thank you all for being a part of this remarkable adventure.

With deepest gratitude,
Shubnum

SOURCES

1. **Website:** https://za.pinterest.com/living8496/joy-vs-happiness/

2. **Website:** www.diffen.com/difference/Happiness_vs_Joy

3. **Website:** https://mediate.com/premarital-mediation-checklist/

4. **Website:** http://www.premaritalcounselling.co.za/

5. **Website:** http://www.dha.gov.za/index.php/civic-services/marriage-certificates

6. **Book:** Subtle Art of Not Giving A F&$k- Mark Manson P63

7. **Quizz:** Online Quizz: https://5lovelanguages.com/quizzes

8. **Article:** Conflict Resolution in Relationships & Couples: 5 Strategies (positivepsychology.com)

9. **Article:** 5 Conflict Management Styles every Manager Must Know (Guide) (valamis.com)

10. **Website:** https://www.attachmentproject.com/blog/four-attachment-styles/

11. **Website:** https://www.mindbodygreen.com/articles/attachment-theory-and-the-4-attachment-styles

12. **Website:** https://www.atlassian.com/blog/teamwork/how-to-navigate-diverse-communication-styles-at-work

13. **Website:** https://thepowermoves.com/communication-styles/

14. **Website:** https://blog.education.nationalgeographic.org/2017/01/20/12-things-we-learned-this-week-8/ultimate-critical-thinking-worksheet/

15. **Article:** What are Enneagram Relationships? Compatibility & Types (marriage.com)

16. **Quizz:** https://enneagramuniverse.com/enneagram/test/

17. **Website:** https://www.enneagraminstitute.com/the-enneagram-type-combinations

18. **Website:** https://www.16personalities.com/free-personality-test

19.**Website**: https://en.wikipedia.org/wiki/Myers%E2%80%93Briggs_Type_Indicator#Differences_from_Jung

20. **Article:** The Top 10 Reasons for Divorce in South Africa | News24

21. **Article**: 100 Fun Questions to Ask Your Spouse On Date Night - LeRyiah Arant

22. **Article:**100 Questions to Ask Each Other Before Marriage (or After, too!) (hautehijab.com)

23. **Article:**100 Questions To Ask Before Marriage For A Stronger Relationship With Your Fiancé | Dr Miriam Torres Brinkmann | YourTango

24. **Website:** https://www.familysavvy.com/how-to-use-swot-to-improve-marriage/

25. **Book:** The Five Agreements – Don Miguel Ruiz

Published by Shubnum, Untangled Love (Pty) Ltd in South Africa, 2023

Copyright Shubnum, 2023

The rights of Shubnum, as the identified author of this work, have been asserted by The Copyright Act 98 of 1978 of South Africa.

A catalogue record for this book is available from the National Library of South Africa.

ISBN: 978-0-7961-4330-3

9 780796 143303

Printed and Distributed by Print on Demand South Africa